First World War
and Army of Occupation
War Diary
France, Belgium and Germany

51 DIVISION
Divisional Troops
Royal Army Medical Corps
1/2 Highland Field Ambulance
29 April 1915 - 31 March 1919

WO95/2858/1

The Naval & Military Press Ltd
www.nmarchive.com
Published in association with The National Archives

Published by

The Naval & Military Press Ltd

Unit 10 Ridgewood Industrial Park,

Uckfield, East Sussex,

TN22 5QE England

Tel: +44 (0) 1825 749494

www.naval-military-press.com

www.nmarchive.com

This diary has been reprinted in facsimile from the original. Any imperfections are inevitably reproduced and the quality may fall short of modern type and cartographic standards.

© Crown Copyright
Images reproduced by permission of The National Archives, London, England, 2015.

Contents

Document type	Place/Title	Date From	Date To
Heading	WO95/2858 51 Div 1/2 Highland F.A May 15-May 19		
Heading	51st Division 1-2nd Highland Fld Ambulance May 1915-1919 Mar		
Heading	51st Div May 1915 1/2nd Highland Field Ambulance Vol I		
Heading	War Diary Of 1/2nd Highland Field Ambulance From 29/4/15 To 31st May 1915 (Volume 1)		
War Diary	Bed Ford	29/04/1915	29/04/1915
War Diary	Southampton	30/04/1915	30/04/1915
War Diary	Havre	01/05/1915	02/05/1915
War Diary	Robecq	03/05/1915	13/05/1915
War Diary	Strazeele	14/05/1915	18/05/1915
War Diary	Vielle Chapelle	19/05/1915	19/05/1915
War Diary	X.3.a	21/05/1915	21/05/1915
War Diary	Les Choquaux	27/05/1915	27/05/1915
War Diary	La Pierre Au Beure	31/05/1915	31/05/1915
Heading	51st Division 1/2nd Highland Field Ambulance Vol II June 1915		
Heading	War Diary Of 1/2nd Highland Field Ambulance Royal Army Medical Corps (T.F.) From 1st June 1915 To 30th June 1915 (Volume II)		
War Diary	La Pierre Au Beure	01/06/1915	01/06/1915
War Diary	Locon	11/06/1915	24/06/1915
War Diary	Estaires	26/06/1915	26/06/1915
Heading	51st Division 1/2 Highland Field Ambulance Vol III July 15		
Heading	War Diary Of 1/2nd Highland Field Ambulance Royal Army Medical Corps (T.F) From 1st July 1915 To 31st July 1915 Volume 3		
War Diary	Estaires	01/07/1915	26/07/1915
War Diary	Merville	28/07/1915	29/07/1915
War Diary	Merinc	29/07/1915	31/07/1915
Heading	51st Division August 1915 1/2nd Highland Field Ambulance Vol IV From 1-31.8.15		
Heading	War Diary Of 1/2nd Highland Field Ambulance R.A.M.C. (T.F) From 1st August 1915 To 31st August 1915 (Vol.4)		
War Diary	Warloy	03/08/1915	26/08/1915
Heading	51st Division Sept 1915 1/2nd Highland Field Amb. Vol V		
Heading	War Diary Of 1/2nd Highland Field Ambulance R.A.M.C. T.F From 1st September 1915 To 30th September 1915		
War Diary	In The Field	18/09/1915	18/09/1915
Heading	51st Division 1/2nd Highland Fd Amb. Nov 1915 Vol VII		
War Diary	Field	07/11/1915	30/11/1915
Heading	51st Div 1/2nd Highland Fd Amb. Dec Vol VIII		
War Diary	Field	23/12/1915	31/12/1915
Heading	51st Div 1/2nd Highd Fd Amb. Jan 1916 Vol IX		

War Diary	Field	10/01/1916	30/01/1916
Heading	51st Division 1/2nd Highland Field Ambulance 2nd Highland Feb March April 1916		
Heading	1/2 High Fd Amb. Feb Vol X		
War Diary	Field	08/02/1916	29/02/1916
Heading	1/2 High Fd Amb Vol XI		
War Diary	Field	01/03/1916	26/03/1916
Heading	1/2 High Fd Amb Vol XII April 1916		
War Diary	Field	19/04/1916	30/04/1916
Heading	51st Div May 1916 1/2nd Highland F. Amb		
War Diary	Field	25/05/1916	31/05/1916
Heading	51st Division June 1916 1/2nd Highland Field Ambulance		
War Diary	Field	01/06/1916	30/06/1916
Heading	51st Division July 1916 1/2 Highland F. Amb		
War Diary	Field	03/07/1916	31/07/1916
Heading	Aug 1916 1/2nd Highland F.A.		
War Diary	Field	01/08/1916	29/08/1916
Heading	51st Div Sept 1916 1/2nd Highland Field Ambulance		
War Diary	Field	01/09/1916	30/09/1916
Heading	51st Division 1/2 Highland Field Amb Oct 1916		
War Diary	Field	01/10/1916	31/10/1916
Heading	51st Div 1/2nd Highland Field Ambulance Mar 1916		
War Diary	Field	01/11/1916	30/11/1916
Heading	51st Div 1/2nd Highland Field Ambulance Dec 1916		
War Diary	Senlis	01/12/1916	28/12/1916
Heading	51st Div 1/2nd Highland Field Ambulance Jan 1917		
War Diary	Field	01/01/1917	29/01/1917
Heading	1/2nd Highland Field Ambulance Feb1917		
War Diary	Field	01/02/1917	28/02/1917
Heading	1/2nd Highland Field Ambulance Mar 1917		
War Diary	Field	01/03/1917	31/03/1917
Heading	51st Div 1/2nd Highland F.A. April 1917		
War Diary	Field	01/04/1917	30/04/1917
Miscellaneous	Summary Of Medical War Diaries		
Miscellaneous	1/2nd High. F.A. 51st Division		
Heading	51st Div 1/2nd Highland F.A. May 1917		
War Diary	Field	02/05/1917	30/05/1917
Miscellaneous	Summary Of Medical War Diaries		
Heading	1/2nd Highland F.A. June 1917		
War Diary	Field	01/06/1917	30/06/1917
Miscellaneous	Summary Of Medical War Diaries Of 1/2nd Highland F.A.		
Heading	1/2nd Highland F.A. July 1917		
War Diary	Field	01/07/1917	30/07/1917
Heading	Summary Of Medical War Diaries Of 1/2nd Highland F.A.		
Heading	1/2nd Highland F.A. Aug 1917		
War Diary	Field	01/08/1917	29/08/1917
Heading	1/2nd Highland F.A. Sept 1917		
War Diary	Field	01/09/1917	30/09/1917
Heading	1/2nd Highland F.A. Oct 1917		
War Diary	Field	03/10/1917	31/10/1917
Heading	1/2nd Highland F.A. Nov 1917		
War Diary	Montenescourt	01/11/1917	17/11/1917
War Diary	Field	18/11/1917	30/11/1917

Heading	1/2nd Highland F.A. Dec 1917		
War Diary	Field	01/12/1917	31/12/1917
Heading	1/2nd Highland F.A. Jan 1918		
War Diary	Beugny	01/01/1918	21/01/1918
War Diary	Achiet-Le-Grand	23/01/1918	29/01/1918
Miscellaneous	1/2nd Highland Field Ambulance R.A.M.C., T.F.	25/01/1918	25/01/1918
Heading	1/2nd Highland F.A. Feb 1918		
War Diary	Achiet-Le-Grand	01/02/1918	12/02/1918
War Diary	Bihucourt	13/02/1918	28/02/1918
Miscellaneous	IV Corps Medical School		
Heading	March 1918 1/2 High F.A.		
War Diary	Field	01/03/1918	31/03/1918
Heading	1/2nd Highland Field Ambulance Apr 1918		
War Diary	Annezin	01/04/1918	04/04/1918
War Diary	Field	04/04/1918	30/04/1918
Heading	1/2nd Highland F.A. May 1918		
War Diary	Fontes	01/05/1918	05/05/1918
War Diary	Field	05/05/1918	31/05/1918
Heading	1/2nd High F.A. June 1918		
War Diary	Aubigny	01/06/1918	30/06/1918
Heading	1/2nd High F.A. July 1918		
War Diary	Aubigny	01/07/1918	17/07/1918
War Diary	Field	17/07/1918	31/07/1918
Heading	1/2nd High F.A. Aug 1918		
Miscellaneous	Cover For Documents. Nature Of Enclosures.		
Miscellaneous	British Salonika Force War Diary		
War Diary	Field St. Imoges	01/08/1918	06/08/1918
War Diary	Field Cambligneul	06/08/1918	22/08/1918
War Diary	Field	23/08/1918	31/08/1918
Miscellaneous	1/2nd Highland Field Ambulance R.A.M.C.T.F.		
Heading	1/2nd High F.A. Sept 1918		
War Diary	St. Catherine	01/09/1918	13/09/1918
War Diary	Ouy Servins	13/09/1918	21/09/1918
War Diary	Gouy-Servins	22/09/1918	30/09/1918
War Diary	Maroiuil	30/09/1918	30/09/1918
Miscellaneous	Contents Of Emergency Limber Wagon	30/09/1918	30/09/1918
Heading	1/2nd Highland F.A. Oct 1918		
War Diary	Maroeuil	01/10/1918	13/10/1918
War Diary	Escaudoeuvres	13/10/1918	31/10/1918
Heading	1/2nd High F.A. Nov 1918		
War Diary	Thun-St-Martin	01/11/1918	20/11/1918
War Diary	Iwuy	21/11/1918	30/11/1918
Heading	1/2nd Highland F.A. Dec 1918		
War Diary	Iwuy	01/12/1918	21/12/1918
War Diary	Bois-Du-Luc	24/12/1918	31/12/1918
Heading	51 Div 1/2nd Highland F.A. Jan 1919		
War Diary	Bois-Du-Luc	06/01/1919	30/01/1919
Heading	1/2nd Highland Field Amb Feb 1919		
War Diary	Bois Du Luc	08/02/1919	27/02/1919
Heading	1/2nd High F.A. Mar 1919		
War Diary	Bois-Du-Luc	01/03/1919	31/03/1919

WO95/2858
51 Div
1/2 Highland F.A
May '15 — Mar '19

51ST DIVISION

1-2ND HIGHLAND FLD AMBULANCE
MAY 1915-~~DEC 1918~~
1919 MAR

51st Div.

121/5444
9 May 1915

131/5444

1/2nd Highland Field Ambulance = 2nd. Highland.

Col L.

Ans

CONFIDENTIAL

WAR DIARY

o/-

1/2nd HIGHLAND FIELD AMBULANCE

From 29/4/15 to 31st May 1915

(Volume 1)

Army Form C. 2118.

WAR DIARY
or
INTELLIGENCE SUMMARY.
(Erase heading not required.)

1/2nd HIGHLAND FIELD AMB ce

51st (HIGHLAND) DIVISION

Instructions regarding War Diaries and Intelligence Summaries are contained in F. S. Regs., Part II. and the Staff Manual respectively. Title pages will be prepared in manuscript.

Place	Date	Hour	Summary of Events and Information	Remarks and references to Appendices
BEDFORD	29/4/15	10.45 am	Received orders to entrain for E.Z. at 12 midnight	T.K.
Southampton	30/4/15	7.30 am	1st Trainload arrived at S. Docks	
		9.15 am	2nd Trainload arrived at S. Docks	
			8 officers and 105 hrs embarked on "Golden Eagle" = 2 officers, remainder grooms, all vehicles and horses on the "Mount Temple". Left SOUTHAMPTON 7 pm "Mount Temple" [P.K.]	T.K.
HAVRE	1/5/15	10 am	disembarked at HAVRE, "Golden Eagle" having disembarked at 7 am.	T.K.
		11 pm	Marched to Rest Camp No 5, & remained there until 11 pm, when moved off to Point-3.	T.K.
	2/5/15	4.19 am	Left HAVRE in one train; arrived at MONTEROLIER-BUCHY at 9 pm : at ABBEVILLE at 5 pm : ST. OMER at 11.50 pm.	T.K.
ROBECQ	3/5/15	8 am	Arrived at ROBECQ by march route, having detrained at MERVILLE — Billeted in Commune School. Opened one Section in Commune School, clearing meanwhile to No 4 Evacuating clearing Stn. LILLERS.	T.K.
			Attached to 1st Infantry Bde, 1st Highland Division.	
ROBECQ	8/5/15	10.30 pm	Received orders to be ready to move on an hour's notice after 6 am 9th inst.	T.K.
ROBECQ	9/5/15	6 am	Packed up & ready to move. Stood by all day.	T.K.
ROBECQ	10/5/15		21 motor ambulance cars, 3 motor lorries, 2 motor cars, 3 motor cycles for use of Highland Divisnl Field Amb Cos arrived at our HQrs; instructions to be taken on my charge meantime, with personnel M.T.	T.K.

1577 Wt. W10791/1773. 500,000 1/15 D. D. & L. A.D.S.S./Forms/C. 2118.

WAR DIARY
or
INTELLIGENCE SUMMARY.

(Erase heading not required.)

Army Form C. 2118.

Instructions regarding War Diaries and Intelligence Summaries are contained in F. S. Regs., Part II. and the Staff Manual respectively. Title pages will be prepared in manuscript.

Place	Date	Hour	Summary of Events and Information	Remarks and references to Appendices
ROBECQ	12/5/15		Highland Casualty Clearing Sta. established at LILLERS. Started cleaning to it.	T.K.
"	13/5/15		Started Hot water Baths for Bde.	T.K.
STRAZEELE	14/5/15		Left ROBECQ at 9.30 am by march route for STRAZEELE by MERVILLE and MERRIS — arrived at 4 pm. Men air firm. Transport in good order. Good Hospital in School.	T.K.
"	15/5/15		Motor Transport joined us. 5 wheelers Cars, 2 fords; 1 Capt., 1 Capt., + 13 Pte. (2 Short) 2 motor cycles short.	T.K.
"	18/5/15	7.30 p.m.	Moved by march route for VIEILLE CHAPELLE : 2 Bearer Goddin on duty at S.B.C.	T.K.
VIEILLE CHAP.	19/5/15		arrived all correct at 4 a.m. Bivouaced in field.	T.K.
ELLE X.3-a	21/5/15		moved by Route March via LA COUTURE to present position, arriving 11 p.m.	T.K.
LES CHOQUAUX	27/5/15		moved by Route March via LOCON to LES CHOQUAUX arriving at 5 pm	T.K.
LA PIERRE AU BEURE	31/9/15		" " " to LA PIERRE AU BEURE, arriving 8 p.m. — Withdrew Bearer Subdivisions from S.B.C. and established Adv. Dress. Stn. with C Subdivision at Le HAMEL near FESTUBERT, clearing to 2/1st Field Amb. at LOCON	T.K.
			One "Other ranks" wounded by shell fire at Adv. Dress. Stn.	T.K.

121/5841

June 1915

51/51 W Dixon

121/5871

2nd Highland

1/2nd Highland Field Ambulance

Vol II

Confidential

War Diary of 1/2nd Highland Field Ambulance,
Royal Army Medical Corps, (T.F.)

From 1st June 1915 To 30th June 1915.

(Volume II.)

WAR DIARY
or
INTELLIGENCE SUMMARY.

2nd Highland Field Ambulance

Army Form C. 2118.

Place	Date	Hour	Summary of Events and Information	Remarks and references to Appendices
LA PIERRE AU BEURE	1915 June 11		One Bearer Section at Advanced Dressing Station at LE HAMEL: remainder resting	TK.
LOCON	June 14	2 pm	Took over Hospital at LOCON, for Officers (sick and wounded) and all ranks Infectious.	TK
"	" 15		Opened out hospital for all cases, 114 under canvas, 220 in buildings.	TK
"	"	6 pm	Commenced to receive wounded.	TK
"	" 16	9 am	Received 340 cases since 6 pm.	TK
"	" 17		Fewer wounded arriving. Evacuation going on steadily.	TK
"	" 18	7 am	Last case evacuated, a total of 491.	TK
"	" 24		Warned to move. Brought back bearers and stores from LE HAMEL and FESTUBERT, leaving 2 officers and ten men & sufficient stores to carry on	TK
ESTAIRES	" 26	10.30 am	Took over Hospital in RUE DE COLLEGE, ESTAIRES from 26 K.F.Amb=	TK

T. Kelly Lt.

War Diary

51st Division.

1/2 Highland Field Ambulance

Vol III

July '15

187/62/14

2nd Highland

aws

Confidential.

WAR DIARY

of

1/2nd Highland Field Ambulance, Royal Army Medical Corps (T.F.)

From 1st JULY, 1915   TO 31st JULY, 1915.

VOLUME 3.

Army Form C. 2118.

WAR DIARY
or
INTELLIGENCE SUMMARY.
(Erase heading not required.)

Instructions regarding War Diaries and Intelligence Summaries are contained in F. S. Regs., Part II. and the Staff Manual respectively. Title pages will be prepared in manuscript.

Place	Date	Hour	Summary of Events and Information	Remarks and references to Appendices
	1915			
ESTAIRES	1st July		Took over Divisional Baths at La Gorgue.	T.K.
"	9th		1 ½ Capt & 4 privates arrived as reinforcement from 2/3rd H.F.A.	T.K.
"	16th		Draft of 8 men (New Army) arr. as 1st division.	T.K.
"	25th		Attached 2 officers to act as Medical Retaining Officers at BERGUETTE and LA GORGUE, with one motor ambulance and one orderly each.	T.K.
"	26th	11 am	Handed over Agricultural College, ESTAIRES to 111th Native Fd Ambs; and baths at LA GORGUE to S.E. troops.	T.K.
"	"	3 pm	Moved by route march to FME ROUSSEL, 3 m. north of MERVILLE.	T.K.
MERVILLE	28th	8 p.m.	" " to BERGUETTE STA.	T.K.
—	29th		Entrained at BERGUETTE 0.08 and left at 2.40	T.K.
MÉRINC.t	"		Detrained at MERINCOURT 15.25 and moved into Billets & here.	T.R.
"	31st		Arranged to take over Hospital from French Authorities at WARLOY.	T.K.

51st Division

August 1915.

121/6650

2nd Highland

amo

1/2nd Highland Field Ambulance

Vol IV

from 1 - 31. 8. 15

Confidential.

War Diary
of
1/2nd Highland Field Ambulance, R.A.M.C., (T.F.)

From 1st August, 1915, to 31st August, 1915.

(Vol. 4.)

Army Form C. 2118

WAR DIARY
or
INTELLIGENCE SUMMARY.
(Erase heading not required.)

Instructions regarding War Diaries and Intelligence Summaries are contained in F. S. Regs., Part II. and the Staff Manual respectively. Title pages will be prepared in manuscript.

Place	Date	Hour	Summary of Events and Information	Remarks and references to Appendices
	1915			
WARLOY	Aug 3.		Ambulance moved by march route to WARLOY-BAILLON, and	TK
	Aug 4		took over HÔPITAL-HOSPICE from 16/16 Ambulance (French)	TK
	July 6		Opened as Divisional Rest Station.	TK
	July 9		Started Baths in Basement of hospital — Water supply of heating arranged.	TK
	July 25		Lc. R.J. Main joined for duty	TK
	- 26		British Red Cross Society delivered various stores for Rest station.	TK

121/6973

51st Division

1/2nd Highland Field Amb: 2nd. Highland

for V

Sep / 15

Sep 1915

Confidential

WAR DIARY
of
1/2nd Highland Field Ambulance,
R.A.M.C., T.F.

From 1st September 1915 to 30th September 1915.

Army Form C. 2118.

WAR DIARY
or
INTELLIGENCE SUMMARY.

(Erase heading not required.) Field Amb ℅

1/2nd Northumbld

Place	Date	Hour	Summary of Events and Information	Remarks and references to Appendices
In the Field	1915 Sept. 18		Carpenters of unit preparing Stove for Expn'l; Force Canteen = lavender Room = + Baths and drying Rooms for troops in this village	P.K.

121/7637

5/9/Swain

2nd. Highland

1/2nd Highlands F? Amb.
Nov 1915

Vol VII

Nov '15

Army Form C. 2118.

WAR DIARY
1/2 n.M. HIG(H LAND) D. FIELD. AMB CE
INTELLIGENCE SUMMARY.
(Erase heading not required.)

Place	Date	Hour	Summary of Events and Information	Remarks and references to Appendices
Field	1915 Nov 1		3 pair horses with 3 men and one Sergeant detailed for duty with Divisional R.E. by order of G.O.C.: making a total of 12 horses, 3 G.S. wagons, 10 personnel.	D.K.
Field	Nov 30		Orders to paint out Red Cross on G.S. wagons detailed for duty with R.E.	D.K.

1st Highland F. Amb.
2nd Highland
Dec
vol VIII
12/7930

WAR DIARY
of 1/2 Highland Field Ambulance
INTELLIGENCE SUMMARY.

(Erase heading not required.)

Army Form C. 2118.

Instructions regarding War Diaries and Intelligence Summaries are contained in F.S. Regs., Part II. and the Staff Manual respectively. Title pages will be prepared in manuscript.

Place	Date	Hour	Summary of Events and Information	Remarks and references to Appendices
Field	23/12/15	10.30am	Christmas on a Divisional Rest Station	S.R.
	26/12/15	9 a.m.	Christmas on a Field Ambulance.	S.R.
	28/12/15	10 a.m.	Handed over to 92nd F.A.: no patients left with them except Patrin.	S.R.
	29/12/15	10/1.30	Left MARLOY at 10 a.m. and reached MIRVAUX at 1.15. Men and transport in good condition. Opened an station in Communal School. Billets fair. Water supply Ventzipe. No infectious cases in village.	S.R.
	31/12/15	10 p.m.	Two heavy days work with fatigue parties cleaning up general surroundings of village which has hitherto not been touched.	S.R.

Sandy Rorie
Major
for O.C. 1/1 H.F.A.
on leave.

5/1st-Div

1/2nd High'd: I. Anml.

Sam / vol. IX

2nd Highland

F/221/1

Jan 1916

Army Form C. 2118.

WAR DIARY
or
INTELLIGENCE SUMMARY.
(Erase heading not required.)

1/2nd HIGHLAND FIELD AMBULANCE

Instructions regarding War Diaries and Intelligence Summaries are contained in F. S. Regs., Part II. and the Staff Manual respectively. Title pages will be prepared in manuscript.

Place	Date	Hour	Summary of Events and Information	Remarks and references to Appendices
Field	1916 Jan 10.		Made Billetting Inspection of typing house and shed in MIRVAUX, annual accommodation for men & horses : drew map to scale 1/5000 = "	J.K.
	Jan 12		Accommodation now ready for 38 Officers, 600 men and 60 horses	J.K.
	" 26		do do do 45 " 900 " 140 "	J.K.
			Major RORIE transferred to command accompanying unit	J.K.
	" 30		Village now contains accommodation for 45 Officers, 1200 men, 180 horses, with hospital accommodation for 40 men	J.K.

51st. Division

112nd Highland Field Ambulance
2nd. Highland

Feb.
March } 1916
April 1916

51

1/2 High Ja Amb
   Feb
  Vol X

Army Form C. 2118.

WAR DIARY
or
INTELLIGENCE SUMMARY.
(Erase heading not required.) Field Ambulance

1/2nd Highland Field Ambulance

Instructions regarding War Diaries and Intelligence Summaries are contained in F. S. Regs., Part II. and the Staff Manual respectively. Title pages will be prepared in manuscript.

Place	Date	Hour	Summary of Events and Information	Remarks and references to Appendices
	1916			
Field	Feb 8		Closed at MIRVAUX and proceeded by route march with 152 Infantry Brigade to CORBIE, where remained closed.	P.K.
"	Feb 28		Under orders to move.	P.K.
"	Feb 29		Moved from CORBIE to PIERREGOT	P.K.

1577 Wt.W10791/1773 500,000 1/15 D. D. & L. A.D.S.S./Forms/C. 2118.

51

1/2 High Fd Amb

Vol XI

# WAR DIARY or INTELLIGENCE SUMMARY.

(Erase heading not required.)

1/2nd Highland Field Ambulance

Army Form C. 2118.

Place	Date	Hour	Summary of Events and Information	Remarks and references to Appendices
Field	1916 Mar 1.		Unit moved to RAINNEVILLE, and opened out.	F.K.
"	" 6		" " to GEZAINCOURT	F.K.
"	" 9		" " to IVERGNY	F.K.
"	" 10		" " to AUBIGNY + reported to D.D.M.S. XVII Corps.	F.K.
"	" 11		Opened as Temporary Casualty Clearing Station pentHuts of the Hôpital d'Evacuation at AUBIGNY.	F.K.
"	" 14.		No 30 C.C. Sta. took over at AUBIGNY and this unit moved to HAUTE AVESNES, leaving a strong section to cooperate with No 30 C.C.S.	F.K.
"	" 17		unit less section at AUBIGNY moved to BERLES	F.K.
"	" 20		Took over Advanced Dressing Station at AUX RIETZ, with Collecting post "Poste Centrale" and annex parties at 4 regimental aid posts, and motor ambulance park at MARŒUIL	F.K.
"	" 26		Attached a party of 1 N.C.O. and 12 men to enlarge dugouts for patients at AUX RIETZ	O.K.

51
Dis

1/2 High^{ld} F^d Amb

Vol XII

April 1916

COMMITTEE FOR
MEDICAL HISTORY OF THE WAR

Army Form C. 2118.

Vol 12

WAR DIARY
or
INTELLIGENCE SUMMARY.

(Erase heading not required.) 1/2nd Highland Field Ambulance.

Place	Date	Hour	Summary of Events and Information	Remarks and references to Appendices
Field	1916 Apr 19		Reported on trials of MOLINE'S Stretcher — carrier & spring allows lateral oscillation & also with heavy man allows stretcher to touch wheels — In one section, shock transf'd to carrier. Wheels are same width (16 inches)	JK
"	Apr 30		Reported on one wheeled stretcher carrier and on Toboggan & on wheel suffic'nt to get round corners and under curves. Stretcher receivers are being constructed in trenches at 150 yards distance from each other, to allow stretcher cases to be lowered, for [strikethrough] adjustment of dressings, & not changing bearers: These are 10 feet long by 3 feet deep, with low roofs to not let the stretcher on, & have corrugated iron roofs	JK JK

51st Div

112nd Highland F. Amb.

May 1915.

COMMITTEE FOR THE
MEDICAL HISTORY OF THE WAR
Date 26 JUN 1915

WAR DIARY
INTELLIGENCE SUMMARY

Army Form C. 2118.

Vol 13

1/2nd Highland Field Ambulance

Place	Date	Hour	Summary of Events and Information	Remarks and references to Appendices
FIELD	25/6	11.p.m	MAJOR D. RORIE took over command of the Ambulance.	
	31/6	6.p.m.	The advanced dressing stations at AU RIETZ and NEUVILLE ST VAAST were taken over by the 1/2 H.F.A. from the 75. F.A., who are acting O and P echelon.	

51st Division

1/2nd Highland Field Ambulance.

June, 1916

COMMITTEE FOR THE
MEDICAL HISTORY OF THE WAR
Date 19 OCT. 1915

Army Form C. 2118.

WAR DIARY
or
INTELLIGENCE SUMMARY.   1/2 Highland Field Ambulance

(Erase heading not required.)

Place	Date	Hour	Summary of Events and Information	Remarks and references to Appendices
FIELD	1/6		Moved from BERLES at 6 p.m. reaching ECOIVRES at 9.30 p.m. Taking over from 7 S.F.A. Weather fine, billets good; no disease amongst civil population; water supply excellent. Opened our section in village school to local area troops.	S.R.
	2/6		Sick. General sanitation of village poor; dung heaps and refuse heaps galore. Busy all day with fatigue cleaning up, constructing incinerator, deep trench latrines, ash urinals re-siting and re use of hospital. Took over Collecting Post in MAROEUIL from 2/1 F.A. Capts BRUCE and STEPHEN re-	S.R.
	3/6		-lieved Capts MELVIN and STEWART at A.D.S. French M.O. asked for medical attendance for 40 French Prisoners at A.C.Q. for a few days. Granted. Tables and benches made for mens' toilette.	S.R.
	4/6		Very short handed for mandatory fatigues owing to many men at A.D.S.	S.R.
	6/6		Went over R.A.P.S. in M.N.O.P. sector and saw M.O.'s there. Brought up 41 French sick from ACQ to hos-	S.R.
	9/6		-pital. Shed at ACQ has been broken into and partially looted by troops tine. Used by front house and, cold and windy, disturbing civils and Sunday mg: work. Capts WALLACE and BROWNE relieved Capts BRUCE and STEPHEN at A.D.S.	S.R.
	16/6		First fine day. Got permission from A.D.M.S. to use billets three from AUX RIETZ to QUARRIES by daylight when men as a/r training camp.	S.R.
	21/6		Arranged for billets (sic) at AUX RIETZ to be marked /in R.A.M.C. one only as pioneers had their mains, and Sketches given them.	S.R.

Army Form C. 2118.

WAR DIARY
or
INTELLIGENCE SUMMARY.
(Erase heading not required.)

1/2 Highland Field Ambulance

Place	Date	Hour	Summary of Events and Information	Remarks and references to Appendices
FIELD	22/6		Undertook Sanitary Supervision of villages billets and made various suggestions to Town Major.	SR
	23/6		Capt STEPHEN and Lt CUNNINGHAM, Leftward attacked, relieving Capt STEWART and Lt HENDERSON at A.D.S. Thurso and tomorrow pair at 4.30 – 5.30. A.M.	SR
	26/6		Handed over billets, Erie AUX RIETZ – QUARRIES. 4 billets down take hove, 1 at NEU- VILLE CO1/VAST and 1 at AUX RIETZ. Signboards pointed to AID POSTS, COLLECTING POSTS and A.D.S.	SR SR
	28/6		C. Section of 2/4 London F.A. arrived for instruction: 3 Officers and 65 other ranks.	SR
	29/6		2 Officers and 48 other ranks detailed through aid posts, collecting posts and A.D.S.	SR
	30/6		Weather of past week Sultry and wet.	SR

51st Division

112 Highland F. Amb.

July 1916

Doc 15 (2). Army Form C. 2118.

1/2 HIGHLAND FIELD AMBULANCE
R.A.M.C. T.

WAR DIARY
or
INTELLIGENCE SUMMARY.
(Erase heading not required.)

Instructions regarding War Diaries and Intelligence Summaries are contained in F. S. Regs., Part II. and the Staff Manual respectively. Title pages will be prepared in manuscript.

Vol / 5

Place	Date	Hour	Summary of Events and Information	Remarks and references to Appendices
FIELD	3/7/16		Constructed 4 corrugated iron incinerators for use of Town Major to be moved from place to place in village to destroy rubbish heaps & accumulations. Weather of last 3 days fine and warm.	S.R.
	5-7/7/16		Section of 2/4 London F.A. moved out and section of 2/6 came in. Distributed flies as before.	
			Completed Sanitary map of ECOIVRES showing all middens, refuse heaps, latrines, gipsy attention, and handed over to Town Major to take copy and necessary action.	S.R.
	6/7/16		Weather last 3 days thunder storms usually and very sultry. Capt. STEPHEN down with P.U.O.	S.R.
	9/7/16		Section of 2/6 London F.A. moved out and section of 2/5" came in. Distributed as before.	S.R.
	11/7/16			S.R.
	13/7/16		Capt. STEPHEN Evacuated to 42 C.C.S. AUBIGNY.	S.R.
	15/7/16		Unit moved to ACQ handing over at ECOIVRES to 2/4 London F.A. Unit left ACQ at 9. a.m. and moved by HAUTES-AVESNES — HAGARCQ — AVESNES LE COMTE — GRAND-RULLECOURT to IVERGNY. Warm day and fine weather. Men in bivouacs and village School.	S.R.
	16/7/16		Unit left IVERGNY at 10. a.m. and proceeded by LUCHEUX — DOULLENS to CANDAS.	S.R.
	18/7/16		Rests two days at CANDAS overhauled Equipment, inspected gas helmets rc.	S.R.
	19/7/16		Unit left CANDAS at 5.30/a.m. and moved by VALHEREUX — NAOURS to TIEFFELLES arriving at 1.30. a.m. Billets poor and arrangements for same bad. Weather dry and warm.	S.R.

Army Form C. 2118.

WAR DIARY
or
INTELLIGENCE SUMMARY. 1/2 HIGHLAND FIELD AMBULANCE
(Erase heading not required.)

Instructions regarding War Diaries and Intelligence Summaries are contained in F. S. Regs., Part II. and the Staff Manual respectively. Title pages will be prepared in manuscript.

Place	Date	Hour	Summary of Events and Information	Remarks and references to Appendices
FIELD	20/7/16		Unit left FLESSELLES at 6 a.m. and moved by VILLERS-BOCAGE — ALLONVILLE — QUERRIEUX — LA BOUSSOYE — BONNAY — HEILLY to RIBEMONT, a 20 mile march. Under trying conditions of heat and dust.	F.R
	21/7/16		Reorganized and checked wagon loads in view of moving into action. Overhauled supplies of dressing splints &c. Unit paraded at 8 p.m. to RIBEMONT and immediately took over Main Dressing Station in Chateau and large barn of Mairie farm as a going concern from 101 F. Amb. Very suitable for work: barn fitted with electric light. Sent 2 bearer subdivisions under CAPT. BROWNE and CAPT STEWART to take over A.D.S at BLACK HUT. Busy all night with heavy stream of casualties.	F.R
	22/7/16		Busy all day with continued admission of casualties. 3 men killed and 8 wounded at BLACK HUT: first deaths in action since sent came out — WILK killed, VEITH and 6 wounded and now 40 below strength. A.D.S BLACK HUT shaken and so untenable Y CAPT BROWNE with party at MARIETZ.	S.R
	23/7/16		Ships a bit slacker. Pte WOLFLEY motor ambulance hit and driver and wagon orderly wounded.	S.R
	25/7/16		Bodies of men killed on 22.7.16 buried at MERICOURT. Casualties two. Another man killed at [struck through] named MARIETZ — QUARRY. Sergt ROGERS seriously wounded and another man mortally wounded —	S.R

1577 Wt. W10791/1773 500,000 1/15 D. D. & L. A.D.S.S./Forms/C. 2118.

Army Form C. 2118.

WAR DIARY
or
INTELLIGENCE SUMMARY.
(Erase heading not required.)

Dec 15 (3) 1/2 HIGHLAND FIELD AMBULANCE
RAMC.

Place	Date	Hour	Summary of Events and Information	Remarks and references to Appendices
FIELD	26/7/16		2 men reported Field last night near QUARRY. Unit moved at 6.30. 1 km to BECORDEL. Total number of Casualties dealt with at Main Dressing Station was 1806. 2 men left old Main-Court as fixed overstore until taken over as Advanced Dressing Station. Said officer absent DERNANCOURT to assist at Main Dressing Station there, reporting to O.C. 132 A-	
	27/7/16		Capt STEPHEN reported unit today from 42 COS MIRGNY.	SR
	29/7/16		Capt METHAM evacuated sick. More casualties at A.D.S.	SR
	30/7/16		Went up to A.D.S QUARRY in person to see progress made by engineers in partially it. Road almost impossible for motors. Evening road reports impassable + Sent out 3 horse ambulances hoping to work QUARRY to road bend to mile this side. Allowed then transferred to motor ambulance wagons here and 12th back to BECORDEL ADS. Road to be mended by engineers	SR
	31/7/16		Worst part of road reported NOW mended. Horse arrangement with ambulance wagons on last night. Horse Casualties amongst personnel. Total number men taken Sheep/Wt. 170 - casualties for last 10 days very warm and dry. For last 4 days flies have been much in evidence.	SR- SR

Dawstrome
Lt Col O C 1/2 HFA

Aug 1916.

1/2nd Highland F.A.

COMMITTEE FOR THE
MEDICAL HISTORY OF THE WAR
Date -5 OCT. 1915

WAR DIARY
or
INTELLIGENCE SUMMARY

Army Form C. 2118.

1/2 HIGHLAND FIELD AMBULANCE

(Erase heading not required.)

Instructions regarding War Diaries and Intelligence Summaries are contained in F.S. Regs., Part II. and the Staff Manual respectively. Title pages will be prepared in manuscript.

Place	Date	Hour	Summary of Events and Information	Remarks and references to Appendices
FIELD	1.8.16		Weather oppressively warm and everything covered with dust.	SR
	2.8.16		Inspected road MAMETZ – QUARRY. The early shelled area at band this side QUARRY now passable. At QUARRY personnel have new pot & fairly good dugouts on slope beyond. Reinforcement of 13 arrived from Base; General Swete unfit for duty.	SR
	3.8.16		Lt McArthur RAMC (TC) temporarily attached for duty. Unit now 47 under strength.	SR
	4.8.16		Capt MEIGHAN RAMC (TF) attached for duty. Still very warm, dusty weather.	SR
	6.8.16		Very warm day. Moved from BECORDEL at 10 a.m. by MEAULTE – DERNANCOURT to E 13 C (ref. map of ALBERT 1/40,000). Unit bivouacked in field there on hill – tof our working parties to DERNANCOURT. Crossers made by unit erected over grown by Pts LUMSDEN, MCINTOSH and DONALDSON at RECORDEL.	SR
	8.8.16	4.30pm	Major MCINTOSH with Capts. BROWNE and MEIGHAN and transport left to proceed by road to SOREL otherwise to move by train at H.15 p.m. for LONG PRE. R.T.O. forced him to entraining	SR
	9.8.16		at 9 p.m. Actually entrained 10 p.m. at EDGE HILL	SR
	10.8.16		Train left EDGE HILL at 2 a.m. LONG PRE 8 a.m. Marched 7 Kilos to SOREL. Men bivouacked in orchard. Clean village with good water supply from deep well.	1
	12.8.16		Marched to PONT-REMY and entrained here for STEENBECQUE, thereafter marching	SR

Army Form C. 2118.

WAR DIARY

INTELLIGENCE SUMMARY. 1/2 HIGHLAND FIELD AMB CE

(Erase heading not required.)

Place	Date	Hour	Summary of Events and Information	Remarks and references to Appendices
FIELD	12.8.16		to BLAIRINGHEM. Men billeted in barns: transport in DISTILLERY yard.	S.R.
	13.8.16		Capt MALLACE and advance party sent to ARMENTIERES to report to O.C. 1 NZ F.A. at MATERNITY HOSPITAL there.	S.R.
	14.8.16		Transport under Major McINTOSH left at 3.a.m. 1st NZFA ARMENTIERES with 154 Bde. Dismounted personnel left BLAIRINGHEM at 1:30, marched to EBLINGHEM and entrained for STEENWERCK thereafter marching to NZ Divisional R.S. LESTRADES.	S.R.
	15.8.16		Party left at 9.A.m. to take over A.D.S at BRICKFIELD, CHAPELLE D'ARMENTIERES. Party left at 2.p.m. to take over M.D.S. at MATERNITY HOSPITAL. Rest of unit left at 5: reaching ARMENTIERES at 7.p.m. at which time the town was being shelled. Men sent to billet INSTITUTE ST JUDE, RUE DENIS PAPIN in Lorries and military, over 40 being brought into M.D.S.; ANZAC, M.D., French & Belgian, Civilian and military, over 40 being brought into M.D.S.; ANZAC, M.D., French & Belgian.	S.R. S.R.
	16.8.16		CAPT MEIGHAN (accidentally) sustained fracture fibula, left.	S.R.
	18.8.16		CAPT MEIGHAN evacuated to No 2 C.C.S BAILLEUL Cpl A.E. WILSON and Pte SCORGIE awarded military medal for work at SOMME	S.R.
	19.8.16		MAJOR D.E. DICKSON RAMC (TF) temporary attached for duty with unit.	S.R.

1577 Wt.W10791/1773 500,000 1/15 D. D. & L. A.D.S.S./Forms/C. 2118.

WAR DIARY

INTELLIGENCE SUMMARY. 1/2 HIGHLAND FIELD AMBULANCE

Army Form C. 2118.

Place	Date	Hour	Summary of Events and Information	Remarks and references to Appendices
FIELD	23.4.16		Capt. STEWART R.A.M.C. (T.C.) left for England on termination of contract and shortly afterwards	SR
	29.8.16		A.T.-Typhus T.A.B. inoculation of unit commenced.	SR
	25.8.16		" " " continued.	SR
	26.8.16		C Section under MAJOR McINTOSH proceeded to 154 Inf Bde Camp, BAIZIEUX to open	SR
			for Relief of Bde.	
	28.8.16		Sandbagging roof of ADS at BRICKFIELD	SR
	29.8.16		CAPT STEWART awarded military Cross and Sergt. FRASER R.D.C.M. for work at SOMME.	SR

F. Rorie
Lt Col
HFA.
O.C. 1/2
31.8.16.

51st Div

1/2nd Highland Field Ambulance.

Sept. 1916

COMMITTEE FOR THE
MEDICAL HISTORY OF THE WAR
Date 26 OCT. 1915

Army Form C. 2118.

WAR DIARY
or
INTELLIGENCE SUMMARY. 1/2 HIGHLAND FIELD AMBS
(Erase heading not required.)

Place	Date	Hour	Summary of Events and Information	Remarks and references to Appendices
Field	1.9.16		Capt G.S. MELVIN left to attend Gas school at OXELEARE.	SR
	2.9.16		Capt R.T. BRUCE went up to A.D.S. of 69 F.A. at BREWERY on ARMENTIERES - PLOEG STEERT ROAD. Went with him to inspect and then moved R.A.P's 4, 5, & 6. A.D.S. & posts on milk cotter 6.20 on invitation for 40 lying cases.	SR
	3.9.16.		Party of 2 NCO's and 18 men detailed from C. Section at Hq. Bde. Training Camp went to BREWERY ADS and RAP'S 4 and RAP'S 4, 5, & 6. Capt BROOME with C. Section took this party. Went to NIEPPE School for night. Capt MELVIN returning from Gas School Lt. MAC-ARTHUR struck off strength on leaving for XIII Corps.	SR
	4.9.16		Took over Main Dressing Station from 69 F.A. at PONT DE NIEPPE with C. Section under Capt WALLACE. Two parties at ADS and NIEPPE School. Major McINTOSH returned to ARMENTIERES. Town heavily shelled in afternoon. Capt HENDERSON relieved at BRICKFIELD ADS with P.U.O.	SR
	5.9.16		Town shelled again in evening. Attempt at other enemies with gas masks tried. Corpl. LAING & Lcpl BRUCE of this unit evacuated with P.S.W. Capt McMURTRIE ordered for duty.	SR
	6.9.16		Some heavy enemy shelling of the town and several casualties admitted. NIEPPE also shelled. Aeroplanes dropped bombs in afternoon, on man killed.	SR

1577 Wt. W10791/1773 500,000 1/15 D. D. & L. A.D.S.S./Forms/C. 2118.

Army Form C. 2118.

WAR DIARY
or
INTELLIGENCE SUMMARY.   1/2 HIGHLAND FIELD AMB.
(Erase heading not required.)

Instructions regarding War Diaries and Intelligence Summaries are contained in F.S. Regs., Part II. and the Staff Manual respectively. Title pages will be prepared in manuscript.

Place	Date	Hour	Summary of Events and Information	Remarks and references to Appendices
FIELD	7.9.16		Handed over Main Dressing Station at PONT DE NIEPPE, hospital accommodation at NIEPPE and BREWERY ADS to 1/3 F.A. Town shelled in evening. Two shells landing on main billets at PENSIONNAT ST JUDE.	STR
	8.9.16		Capt. HENDERSON evacuated with P.U.O. Sandbagged the roof of cellars at main billets and also roof of cellars occupied by nurses at back of buildings and propped the ceiling. Town shelled again in evening.	STR
	9.10.16		Major MCINTOSH with Capt BRUCE returned to Hq. Got Training Camp. Met Col Leslie.	STR
	13.10.16		Sandbagged and propped cellar at MATERNITY HOSPITAL	STR
	15.10.16		12 cubic beams, 40 Stalchion, 500 lanthils and 500 short D bearing extra sent up to ADS. BRICKFIELD, walk 0.57. Horse Motor Ambulance began in view of probable Mess. Com. Prewed erecting a "Prenet" (mortar with sandbags) dug out at corner of MATERNITY HOSPITAL Grounds. Working also at horse-standings and shelter at Standard Lines.	STR
	19.10.16		Working at dug out and hrs. erecting Kitchen windows to keep out flies which have been very numerous and troublesome. Fair weather past couple weeks in spite of formalis prophysis.	STR
	21.5.16		Taken to sr. Dug out finished.	STR

1577 Wt.W10791/1773 500,000 1/15 D.D.&L.   A.D.S.S./Forms/C. 2118.

Army Form C. 2118.

WAR DIARY
or
INTELLIGENCE SUMMARY.
(Erase heading not required.)

1/2 HIGHLAND FIELD AMBCE

Place	Date	Hour	Summary of Events and Information	Remarks and references to Appendices
Field	25.5.16		Lt. & Q.M. GIBBON evacuated to C.C.S. TROIS ARBRES with P.U.O. with two Section of Inf: Bde Camp moved to LA CRECHE.	
	26.5.16		Lt. FREEMAN lecturing officers 1st 2nd & 3rd with min:	
	30.9.16		Capt: MACINTOSH with Capt BRUCE and Section of Infantry Brigade Training Camp returned back at LA CRECHE.	

David Rorie
Lt Col. RAMC
O.C. 1/2 H.F.A.

149/1788

51st Division.

1/2. Highland Field Amb.

Oct 1916

Army Form C. 2118.

WAR DIARY
INTELLIGENCE SUMMARY.
(Erase heading not required.)

Instructions regarding War Diaries and Intelligence Summaries are contained in F. S. Regs., Part II. and the Staff Manual respectively. Title pages will be prepared in manuscript.

1/2 HIGHLAND FIELD AMBULANCE.

Vol 18

Place	Date	Hour	Summary of Events and Information	Remarks and references to Appendices
FIELD	1.10.16		Transport left at 1.a.m. for BAILLEUL main station and personnel at 2.30.a.m. Entrained and left BAIL at 5.26.a.m. for DOULLENS. Thence marched to GEZAINCOURT. Billets for men. Weather cold and dull.	
	2.10.16		Unit moved at 10.a.m. by FRESCHVILLERS – SARTON – AUTHIE – nr. 152 Bde to BOIS DE WARNIMONT. Rang had boys and ammunition parked. Billets in huts in wood. Lt FREEMAN reconnoitred field with R.U.O. to DOULLENS upon instructions. Lt. Col. M. GIBBON reconnoitred sites with R.U.O. to DOULLENS from BOIS DE WARNIMONT.	
	3.10.16		After a very bad and cold night unit moved to BUS LES ARTOIS taking over M.D.S. huts from 132 F.A.. With Capt BRUCE went to 152 Bde over A.D.S. at COLINCAMPS but found it had been handed over on previous day to 5th F.A. Proceeded to and over the Advanced Post at EUSTON. Stood-down by road-side. Lt. Rixon R.A.M.C (T.C) attached for duty.	
	4.10.16		To COLINCAMPS and EUSTON with D.A.D.M.S. and nr. WAGRAM TRENCH to see possible sites for new R.A.P.'s for Regd. Sectn. Fired on by gun near CHAUSSEUR'S HEDGE.	
	5.10.16		Busy with fatigue work at M.D.S. repairing leaking huts, cleaning ground, making pathways, making both horse and latrines. Improved washes and found a slop-mine.	

Army Form C. 2118.

WAR DIARY
INTELLIGENCE SUMMARY. 1/2 HIGHLAND FIELD AMBULANCE

(Erase heading not required.)

Place	Date	Hour	Summary of Events and Information	Remarks and references to Appendices
FIELD	6.10.16		Opened at 10 a.m. to admit wounded from 2/1 H.F.A. A.D.S. at HEBUTERNE. Went up in person with Capt. BRUCE to reconnoitre probable Advanced R.A.P. beyond COIGNCAMPS to PAPIN TRENCH. A track passable 6/8 of the way runs twice NORTHERN AVENUE.	
	7.10.16		Ten figures filled at work with flickering broken tracks and the making passages at M.D.S. Flooring and cementing bath house, digging out trench latrines and fixing in ablution benches with new roof etc. Very wet weather.	
	8.10.16		Got 20 Huns from Cage to assist in road-making. Had a meeting of M.O.'s units to discuss various matters.	
	11.10.16		Left at 4.30 a.m. with 2 M.O.'s units for HEBUTERNE to view A.D.S.'s & R.A. and S.Coy route to and from R.A.P.'s. Very cold and wet.	
	12.10.16		Conference at A.D.M.S. Office of O.i.C.'s F.A. A.D.S. to be at COIGNCAMPS; Advanced post to Reserve Brown at PAPIN and by HOME AVENUE; an advanced Medicine Store at FORT BRIGGS R.A.P. and 2nd R.A.P.'s at CHAUSSEURS HEDGE	
	13.10.16		With 2 officers of 1/2, 3 of 1/3 and the 6 Bearer Sgts. of 1/2 and 1/3 went over evacuation route from in-fused new R.A.P.'s to COIGNCAMPS. HOME AVENUE and PAPIN very badly fouled. Few works Party of 50 men to COIGNCAMPS at 9 a.m. to work under R.E. officers at strengthening and repairing dug outs.	

1577 Wt. W10791/1773 500,000 1/15 D. D. & L. A.D.S.S./Forms/C. 2118.

WAR DIARY
INTELLIGENCE SUMMARY. 1/2 HIGHLAND FIELD AMBULANCE

Army Form C. 2118.

(Erase heading not required.)

Place	Date	Hour	Summary of Events and Information	Remarks and references to Appendices
FIELD	14.10.16		Had one walking wounded case from SAILLY-AU-BOIS to COLINCAMPS and 2 offices 1/2. Road break. Prepared purposes of post at PAPIN end of HOME AVENUE and 1/3 work in progress at CHAUSSEURS HEDGE. Lt RIXON started off strength of unit today. Bath water laid out.	
	15.10.16		Improved work at COLINCAMPS dugouts. Relieved 1/5 F.A. Bureau at FORT BRIGGS. Conference with M.O.'s of 152 Bde in afternoon. Weather drier.	
	16.10.16		Walk ADMS to COLINCAMPS and post at PAPIN end of HOME AVENUE. Work well in hand.	
	17.10.16		Started to take over ADS MAILLY with C.P. at AUCHONVILLERS, and R.A.P.s at BUNKER ROAD, WHITE CITY, TENDERLOIN, II AVENUE, THURLES DUMP and UXBRIDGE ROAD. Went to MAILLY and found the lot built O/C ADS R'ND Ave. Present building at MAILLY and AUCH- ONVILLERS little use for purposes, and as the R.A.P.'s and work done, but a more easily workable line of line than kind. Hoping Kartis in to see flares mentioned except UXBRIDGE ROAD.	
	18.10.16		Had moved to FORCEVILLE, landing our MDS BUS-LES-ARTOIS to 1/42 F.A.- man Lieut-fair: officers in tents. Weather wet. Very heavy rain through night. Went to MAILLY- and AUCHONVILLER. Rather pleased his took right and one man wounded slightly, half A.D.M.S. Later to MAILLY.	
	19.10.16			
	20.10.16		Clear, cold and frosty. Went with R.E. officer to AUCHONVILLERS re work needed there. Stables in country and to the hunting and fabric necessary. Walls of the quadrangle and loose	

WAR DIARY
INTELLIGENCE SUMMARY. 1/2 H.F. AMBULANCE

Army Form C. 2118.

Place	Date	Hour	Summary of Events and Information	Remarks and references to Appendices
FIELD			slept soundly in another part of court yard, though am and fired in. Roof of cellar to be sand bagged and entrance mouth of buildings. BREWERY (BLARNEY HOUSE) to be handed over to unit as A.D.S. Arranged with R.E. officer regarding re-building and properly releasing sandbagging entrances etc. Excellent cellarage and room for expansion. To MAILLY taken with 2 officers of 1/2 to reconnoitre road to BEAUSART for walking wounded and places for Tuesday night. Has been made in afternoon. Working party of 50 at AUCHONVILLERS under Capt BRUCE.	
	21.10.16			
	22.10.16		To AUCHONVILLERS and round R.A.P.'s with D.A.D.M.S. Works fair on well.	
	23.10.16		Round working parties again at M.D.S., C.P. and TENDERLOIN.	
	24.10.16		Inspected work at A.D.S. and C.P.	
	25.10.16		Inspected work at A.D.S. & C.P. Write A.D.M.S. re TENDERLOIN, late walk 2 officers & 1/3 round R.A.P's and evacuation routes. Very wet and muddy. Conference of M.O's. over draft F.A. in afternoon at LEALVILLERS. Found supply of straw run at C.P. and TENDERLOIN and all other stores at MAILLY.	
	26.10.16		Killed 3 officers of 2/1 F.A. round M.D.S. C.P. and R.A.P.'s near Bois Rochester. Seriously wounded. Began moving packings to AUCHONVILLERS.	

WAR DIARY

INTELLIGENCE SUMMARY.

1/2 H.F.AMB 5E

Army Form C. 2118.

Place	Date	Hour	Summary of Events and Information	Remarks and references to Appendices
FIELD	27.10.16		At II AVENUE & down third street, rebuilt shaft in another R.A.P. at BROADWAY. Crew turn with officer of 1/5 R.S. (Pioneers) and fixed on site, & started work at once.	
			IV AVENUE cleaned and front shed boards in places. Took two STRETCHERS and for hospital to clean and widen entrance hole. Weather wet.	
	28.10.16		To MDS rep. all work practically finished - UXBRIDGE ROAD requires work done at once - Weather wet.	
	29.10.16		To ADS, CP, THURLES DUMP and UXBRIDGE ROAD. Received word be done at last place.	
	31.10.16		To ADS, CP, and BROADWAY. Put on a working party of men to finish at BRgty Dugout back and entrance and fit in a perfing door - Shelter for R.A.M.C. personnel at THURLES DUMP requires strengthening as well -	

A. Rouse
Lieut
OC 1/2 H.F.A.-

140/649

51st Div

1/2nd Highland Field Ambulance.

No. 3/10/16

COMMITTEE FOR THE
MEDICAL HISTORY OF THE WAR

Date −3 JAN. 1917

WAR DIARY
INTELLIGENCE SUMMARY.

1/2 HIGHLAND FIELD AMBULANCE

Army Form C-2118.

(Erase heading not required.)

Instructions regarding War Diaries and Intelligence Summaries are contained in F. S. Regs., Part II. and the Staff Manual respectively. Title pages will be prepared in manuscript.

Place	Date	Hour	Summary of Events and Information	Remarks and references to Appendices
FIELD	1.11.16		Wet weather and cold. To MAILLY and AUCHONVILLERS to inspect working parts at take place of sick entrance and exit for cave with road through farmyard. A working party of 30 men at UXBRIDGE ROAD from unit making R.A.P.'s there — 2 dugouts being re-timbered and roof strengthened, with STR front entrances to trench and road. One man wounded and returned to duty here.	
	2.11.16		With D.A.D.M.S. to MAILLY, AUCHONVILLERS, STOCKTON DUMP (Soup Kitchen) and to THURLES DUMP and UXBRIDGE ROAD R.A.P.'s to inspect progress of working parties. Ran to new R.A.P. at BROADWAY. Very wet and muddy. Things well forward.	
	3.11.16		To MAILLY and AUCHONVILLERS.	
	4.11.16		To MAILLY, AUCHONVILLERS, BROADWAY, THURLES, DUMP and UXBRIDGE ROAD with Capt Bruce. Work well in hand. Had to use trenches all the way as things were lively. Very cold and wet. Orders in evening that all operations were in abeyance postponed.	
	5.11.16		High wind and very cold.	
	6.11.16		To MAILLY and AUCHONVILLERS to overhaul stores. Land explosive and rifle fire to south about 11. P.M. — Capt. MEIGHAN and Capt McMURTRIE M.O.'s 1/5 R.Scots down his late to consult about raid tomorrow night by 1/9 R. Scots.	
	7.11.16		To MAILLY WOOD to see O.C. 1/5 R. Scots regarding tonight's raid. Capt MEIGHAN to walk	

WAR DIARY
INTELLIGENCE SUMMARY

Army Form C. 2118.

(Erase heading not required.)

1/2 HIGHLAND FIELD AMBULANCE

Place	Date	Hour	Summary of Events and Information	Remarks and references to Appendices
FIELD	7.11.16		Early at 3.30 A.M. sent relie teams (12) to TENDERLOIN as reserve and an extra car to AUCHONVILLERS. "Zero" now fixed at 11 H. Cold, wet day; very heavy rain.	
	8.11.16		To MAILLY and AUCHONVILLERS to rearrange personnel and check stores.	
	9.11.16		To MAILLY and AUCHONVILLERS. Last night a S.9 landed on roof of flounder-steering chamber and flames off pipe unperturbed cart-house. Food tent of thatches which stood is well. One ocean wounded Head, hand and leg.	
	10.11.16		Z day, now 13th. To MAILLY and AUCHONVILLERS to inform Notre Dame.	
	11.11.16		To MAILLY and AUCHONVILLERS. Preparation finished for 13th. AUCHONVILLERS being shelled freely.	
	12.11.16		To AUCHONVILLERS at 5 A.M. Zero 5:45 A.M. tomorrow. All bearers y P. 1/3 and 2/1 N. Hein. Thailand. All stretcher trolleis loaded at AUCHONVILLERS. Major McINTOSH with CAPT. MALLACE with bearers MEIGHAN with 2nd Subdivision and 20 Reserve Bearers with 40 bearing & Caps at FORCEVILLE : Capt. STEPHEN, MELVIN & BROWNE at MAILLY: Capt BRUCE, AUCHONVILLERS & Caps TORRANCE at TENDERLOIN after infantry attack R.A.S. A good many fax shells and H.E. come over in evening with occasional Right shrapnel.	
	13.11.16 6/7 a.m.		Wounded commenced to come in at J.G.W. and soon became a steady stream on by all day.	
	11 a.m.		Evacuation went on steady from the first. C.P. shelled at 11 A.M. and 2.45 P.M. and	
	11.30 a.m.		had to clear the courtyard of all cars on that occasion. No casualties. German prisoners came	

WAR DIARY
or
INTELLIGENCE SUMMARY

Army Form C.2118.

Place	Date	Hour	Summary of Events and Information	Remarks and references to Appendices
FIELD	13.11.16		Came in successfully at few men and 150 have held up for extra bearers. Led them from STOCKTON DUMP. Sent KITCHEN and 2 fed them in charge of bearers. Fog works nightly and well. Busy time checking reports, running calls for fresh bearers and NOTES on ROAD through AUCHONVILLERS and ROAD to THURLES DUMP and UXBRIDGE ROAD. Fresh shells all day but no casualties enough.	
		7.p.m.	Personnel. Things improved at having no reports numbers coming in.	
	14.11.16		Nothing all night. Things quieter had a constant evacuation. No 1/5 R.H. refused at 3.30.	
		3.30.a.m	As an of in Y RAVINE and Capt APPLETHWAITE 1/3 F.A. passage from 153 Bde re-ports 300 wounded in Y RAVINE. Lt ANDERSON with a bearer sub division of 2/2 SOUTH MIDLAND FIELD AMBULANCE sent up to assist. As had numbers and evacuation going on steadily. Similar message from 152 Bde regarding large numbers of wounded in TENDERLOIN resulted in Capt BEGG with a Bearer Division of 2/1 F.A. going out there who should have been ready for relief. Capt BEGG filled at several men to shell over TENDERLOIN. Sent out Capt VICKERS of 2/2 S. MIDLAND F.A. to replace him and	
		3.45. 6.m	report to me how evacuation was proceeding. Report stated everything satisfactory and that no check had ever occurred. Telegraph with report received from Capt TORRANCE	

WAR DIARY or INTELLIGENCE SUMMARY

Army Form C. 2118.

Place	Date	Hour	Summary of Events and Information	Remarks and references to Appendices
FIELD	14.11.16	6 p.m.	FORD CAR running down BEAUMONT-HAMEL ROAD to Luring - found officers TENDERLOIN ROAD occasionally, but absolutely necessary to relieve the Inf. wounded leaving when conditions of working men returning had. Remains of V.2 killed near WHITE CITY.	
	15.11.16 8 a.m.		Head down to TENDERLOIN (WHITE CITY) and called on B.G.C. 152 Bde to refund on evacuation. Walked out to an about a German R.A.P. in BEAUMONT-HAMEL to head with pride, officer of 1/6 Seaforths, across ravine to right hand bank over BEAUMONT-HAMEL & STATION ROAD. Visited 3 dugouts with German dead and wounded, but some from Surgeon from TENDERLOIN for an advanced post for relief bearers and stores. Enemy snipers and M.Gs fire and 5.9's. German wounded removed. Some not often seen. Reported to Bdy. Divisional M/S and Lieut. S.A.D.M.S. walked back to AUCHONVILLERS and found road blocked in village by Shell-holes and Review there severe road. Lou-working party and Pn in charge of same. AUCHONVILLERS full shelled in afternoon and evening.	
	16.11.16 8 a.m.		Took a horse down in (parts of 1/2 1/s of 5h) down to TENDERLOIN to examine case for evacuating of sg. wounded. Got 30 through in a chiefly stretcher and moving from Chip on to Capt. TORRANCE & BROWNE joined me in afternoon. R.A. R.'s run in STATION ROAD & WAGON ROAD, BEAUMONT HAMEL - further forward Hy can be got Road Keeps	

1577 Wt.W10791/1773 500,000 1/15 D. D. & L. A.D.S.S./Forms/C. 2118.

WAR DIARY
or
INTELLIGENCE SUMMARY

Army Form C. 2118.

Place	Date	Hour	Summary of Events and Information	Remarks and references to Appendices
	17.11.16		Very heavy shelling around WHITE CITY killing a lot of attendants. A.D.M.S. visited pt. Knupff injd. and off duty along with a large number of 32.? Div. Casualties. L. Breig has to send 60 bearers at once to clear Main Aid posts. Reports A.D.M.S. take 2 Officers and 30 Bearers of 32 Div.t Ambulances sent to WHITE CITY which carried on work although had rite to had a rest	
	18.11.16		Still dealing with 32. Div.t Wounded. Route very dangerous especially at WAGON ROAD, STATION ROAD corner.	
	19.11.16	9 am	New round all R.A.P.S, 57 Div. v 32. Div. Zi. MATION & WAGON ROADS to see how evacuation was proceeding. The corner makes a hot spot. Work has been fine. etd. Head to HQ MS to report and take interview Capt. TORRANCE and BROWNE from TENDERLOIN, leaving a M.O. and 24 rubbish bearers to work 12 hourly reliefs with bearers in R.A.P.S. Brangus loads all three men to FORCEVILLE	
	20.11.16		Capt. BROWNE left on leave. Inspecting Stores around from Line	
	21.11.16		Collecting and arranging stores. Capt BRUCE attached from AUCHONVILLERS and Capt MEIGHAN relieved him.	
	22.11.16		Took over MDS FORCEVILLE from 1/3 W.E.C.Div. Open for Dut. Sick and wounded	

… Army Form C. 2118.

WAR DIARY

INTELLIGENCE SUMMARY. 1/2 HIGHLAND FIELD AMBULANCE

(Erase heading not required.)

Instructions regarding War Diaries and Intelligence Summaries are contained in F. S. Regs., Part II. and the Staff Manual respectively. Title pages will be prepared in manuscript.

Place	Date	Hour	Summary of Events and Information	Remarks and references to Appendices
FIELD	23.11.16		Handed over to 2.1st Field Ambulance.	
	24.11.16		All men back from leave today. Capt BRUCE left on leave.	
	26.11.16		Put in holding hands at M.D.S. as 2.1. F.A. left today. Major MACKINTOSH and Capt TORRANCE evacuated to C.C.S. with P.U.O. Capt Wilkinson to hospital	
	27.11.16		Capt MEECHAN detailed as temporary M.O. /c 1/8 A. & S.H. Unit moved at 3.30pm to SENLIS and took over D.R.S. here from 12 Canadian F.A. who left 320 patients and the place in a very untidy condition. Capt MELVIN evac. held with P.U.O. to GEZAINCOURT.	
	28.11.16		Busy cleaning up, varnishing, repairing roads and huts and cleaning out caves.	
	29.11.16		Same work.	
	30.11.16		Capt STEPHEN detailed as temporary M.O. /c II Corps mounted troops. Their horse-men walk 2 officers to carry on work here.	

D. Rorie
Lt Col
O.C. 1/2 H.F.A.

51st Div.

140/900

1/2nd Highland Field Ambulance

Dec 06

COMMITTEE FOR THE
MEDICAL HISTORY OF THE WAR
Date 31 JAN. 1917

WAR DIARY

of 1/2nd Highland Field Ambulance

INTELLIGENCE SUMMARY

Army Form C. 2118.

Place	Date	Hour	Summary of Events and Information	Remarks and references to Appendices
Senlis	1/31.12.16		Working Divisional Rest Station - Average number of patients treated 250 per day.	SR
"	1/31.12.16		Joiners engaged in construction of large dining hut which is now almost completed.	SR
"	1.12.16		Captain BROWNE returned from leave.	SR
"	"		Captain Gavin E. ARGO, 2/1st H.T. Ambulance temp. attd for duty.	SR
"	4.12.16		Captain G. TORRANCE returned for duty from Cas. Clear. Station.	SR
"	6.12.16		Captain R.T. Bruce returned from leave.	SR
"	7.12.16		Extract from Unit orders "Honours & Awards". The General Officer Commanding in Chief has, under authority granted by His Majesty The King, awarded decorations to the undermentioned for gallantry during the operations on 13th November 1916 and subsequent days. Lieutenant Charles TAWSE, Mounted Ambce T.F.	SR
			No. 1436 Private James Stower Sawden HAY - do -	SR
			1911 " "	
"	9.12.16		Captain Walker returned from hospital.	

Army Form C 2118.

Vol 20 (2)

WAR DIARY
of
INTELLIGENCE SUMMARY.
/2nd Highland Field Ambulance.
(Erase heading not required.)

Place	Date	Hour	Summary of Events and Information	Remarks and references to Appendices
Sailly	12.12.16		Major J.F. MACINTOSH. on leave to Scotland 12/22.12.16. Captain G. TORRANCE is detailed as temp. M.O. i/c Amb. & Suth Highrs during the absence of M.O. on leave.	SR
"				SR
"	14.12.16		Extract from Unit Orders:— Honours & Rewards — The General Officer Commanding 51st High. has under authority granted by this HQ gazetted the undermentioned for gallantry during the operations on 13th November 1916. The MILITARY CROSS — Captain HAWTREY WILLIAM BROWNE. /2nd High. Field Ambulance T.F.) Captain S.S. MEICHAN → detailed to attend daily sick	SR
"	16.12.16		of 51st Div Supply Column at Hafoncelle. 3 y.C.O.'s & 36 men detailed for work on "dug outs" at CRIGHTON'S Post.	SR
"	16.12.16			SR
"	17.12.16		Captain J.A. STEPHEN struck off strength on proceeding to report to H.Q. I.G.C.	SR

WAR DIARY
INTELLIGENCE SUMMARY

1/2nd Highland Field Ambulance (R.A.M.C. T.F.) Vol. 20. (3)

Army Form C. 2118

Place	Date	Hour	Summary of Events and Information	Remarks and references to Appendices
Sandis.	18.12.16		Captain S.S. MEIGHAN is detailed as temp. M.O. IV Corps Conv. Park.	OTR
"	"		Captain R.T. BRUCE is detailed as temp. M.O. of 15 Seaforth Highrs.	OTR
"	20.12.16		Lieut. C.E.A. WILSON, RAMC (T.C.) reported for duty from 2/6 M.A.C.	OTR
"	22.12.16		Lieut. C.E.A. WILSON is detailed as temp. M.O. of RFA 252 Brigade.	OTR
"	24.12.16		Capt. A.R. GRANT RAMC (T.F.) reported for duty from 2/1 amb. train.	OTR
"	29.12.16		Captain A.R. GRANT is detailed as temp. M.O. 1/4 Gord. Highrs.	OTR
"	13.12.16		10 men detailed for work on OFFICERS HUTS.	OTR

D. Rorie.
LIEUT. COL., R.A.M.C., T.F.
O.C. 1/2nd HIGHLAND FIELD AMBULANCE

51st Div.

14/1941

1/2nd Highland Field Ambulance.

for 1917

COMMITTEE FOR THE
MEDICAL HISTORY OF THE WAR
Date 13 MAR. 1917

WAR DIARY
1/2 7kgh Field Amb.
INTELLIGENCE SUMMARY.

Army Form C. 2118.
Vol 21 (1)
R.A.M.C.(T)

Place	Date	Hour	Summary of Events and Information	Remarks and references to Appendices
FIELD	1/3-1-17		Capt. Col. A. Ross detailed to act as A.D.M.S. temp, during absence of Col Stanning on leave (SENLIS)	App from
FIELD	4/12-1-17		Working Divisional Rest Station - Average number of patients treated 250 per day.	App from
	4.1.17		Capt. R.D. Bruce returned from temp duty with 1/5 Sea. Highrs.	85 M
	5.1.17		" G.S. Melvin assumed temp medical charge of 68th (C.F.) Artillery Group Hd. Qrs. at Acourt.	85 M
	7.1.17		Capt. G.S. Melvin rejoined unit from Hd Qrs Artillery Group to men detailed to report to C.C.S. 2/1 St.J.Amb. for duty with working party at Brighton Post	85 M
	10.1.17		Capt. G.S. Melvin + 5 O.R. left to take over Decia Ambulance Accommodation at OUVILLE. (Rest Area)	85 M
	11.1.17		15 O.R. left for OUVILLE to assist in taking over accommodation there.	87 M
	12.1.17		Handed over to 5th Fd Amb moved to VAC DE MAISON (1st stage of march to Rest Area)	93 M
	13.1.17		Capt. G. Dorrance detailed as temp. M.O. to 1/7 Royal Highrs.	85 M
	14.1.17		Unit moved to VACQUERIE. (2nd stage of march to Rest Area)	85 M

Army Form C. 2118.

WAR DIARY
1/2 Highland Field Ambulance
INTELLIGENCE SUMMARY
(Erase heading not required.)

Vol. 21 (2)
R.A.M.C.(T)

Instructions regarding War Diaries and Intelligence Summaries are contained in F. S. Regs., Part II. and the Staff Manual respectively. Title pages will be prepared in manuscript.

Place	Date	Hour	Summary of Events and Information	Remarks and references to Appendices
FIELD	15.1.17		Unit moved to NEUF MOULIN (3rd stage of march to Rest Area)	87/M
	16.1.17		" " OUVILLE and took over Rest Station there	87/M
	17.1.17		Capt Meighan detailed to attend Chuile Sect of D.D.M.S. II Corps	87/M
	16/31.1.17		Working Divisional Rest Station at OUVILLE - Average number of patients treated 150 per day.	82/M
	25.1.17		Capt G. Torrance detailed to visit at Sentees Hope Choors	87/M
			& S. Meeun proceeded on leave	80/M
	29.1.17		Lieut Wilson detailed at temp MO - R.B.A 255 Bde	85/M
	1/2.16.1.17		During march to rest area 140 patients were dealt with	

J G MacJabsh
Major
LIEUT. COL., R.A.M.C., T.F.
O.C. 1/2nd HIGHLAND FIELD AMBULANCE

1577 Wt.W10791/1773 500,000 1/15 D. D. & L. A.D.S.S./Forms/C. 2118.

140/1994

1/1st Highland Field Ambulance

COMMITTEE FOR THE
 CAL HISTORY OF THE WAR
Date 4 APR 1917

WAR DIARY
INTELLIGENCE SUMMARY

Army Form C., 2118.

Vol. 22 (1)

Highland Field Ambulance Panel (1)

Place	Date	Hour	Summary of Events and Information	Remarks and references to Appendices
FIELD	1.2.17		At Rest Station OMVILLE & preparing for moving to a New Area.	Vol 2 DR
"	2.2.17		Lieut Colonel RORIE rejoined unit from 1/ADMS 51st Division	DR
"	3.2.17		Lieut Col. RORIE proceeded on leave to Scotland 14.2.17 to 14.2.17.	DR
"	3.2.17		Hancock granted an extension of 7 days.	DR
"	4.2.17		Captain Meighan temply attd 1/6 Gordon Highrs	DR
"	5.2.17		Unit moved to Place D'Armes Camp.	DR
"	5.2.17		Ford Motor Ambulance wrecked at level crossing by train near ST RIQUIER.	DR
"	"		Captain Melvin admitted to No. 11 Gen. Hosp. sick off leave.	DR
"	6.2.17		Unit moved to BOFFLES.	DR
"	7.2.17		Unit moved to HERICOURT.	DR
"	8.2.17		Unit moved to MONCHY-BRETON.	DR
"	9.2.17		Unit moved to CRUCOURT.	DR
"	10.2.17		Unit moved to HAUTE AVESNES and took over Main Dressing Station for Rtes in Front area & Corps Sick	DR

O RORIE
LIEUT. COL., R.A.M.C., T.F.
O.C. 1/2nd HIGHLAND FIELD AMBULANCE

Army Form C. 2118.

WAR DIARY
or
INTELLIGENCE SUMMARY.

1/2nd Highland Field Ambulance (T.) Vol 22 (2)

(Erase heading not required.)

Instructions regarding War Diaries and Intelligence Summaries are contained in F. S. Regs., Part II. and the Staff Manual respectively. Title pages will be prepared in manuscript.

Place	Date	Hour	Summary of Events and Information	Remarks and references to Appendices
FIELD	1/12/14	3.4.	Took over ADS. at ANZIN and collecting posts at MADAGASCAR & LILLE ROAD. During the more from Ouvries to Hants Queenes great difficulty was experienced with transport. (1) Horse transport, owing to the very hard frost & horses were unable to draw the wagons uphill so necessary frequently to be assisted by personnel. (2) Motor transport, owing to the state of the cars & the fact that M.T. of seven workshops, and the Brigade sick which had to be evacuated were sometimes spread over a rather wide area. Sick & wounded dealt with. Average daily sick 60. (including Corps troops) Captain Torrance employed duties with Capt. Grant today attached 1st Gordon Highrs.	SR SR SR SR SR
	13.2.14 28/1/14			

[signature] Marie
LIEUT. COL. R.A.M.C., T.F.
O.S. 1/2nd HIGHLAND FIELD AMBULANCE

WAR DIARY
INTELLIGENCE SUMMARY.

Army Form C. 2118.

1/2 H't Ambulance Dec 22 (3)

France (T.F.)

Place	Date	Hour	Summary of Events and Information	Remarks and references to Appendices
FIELD	18.2.17		Sent Wilson evacuated sick to No. 42 C.C. Stn.	SR
"	19.2.17		L/Cpl Q.M. GIBBON reported for duty.	SR
"	20.2.17		Capt Grant detailed as Coy M.O of RFA 25? Dale in relief of Captain Scott who is attached to this ambulance for a course of instruction on field ambulance work.	SR
"	21.2.17		Working party of 1 Sergt & 10 men sent to Annex a.d.s. to commence work on (D) improving dug outs (E) construction of splinter proof & elephant shelters.	SR
"	22.2.17		Lieut. Wilson returned to duty from No. 2 C.C. Station.	SR
"	23.2.17		Further fatigue party of 1 NCO & 10 men sent for work at A.D.S.	SR

S Rorie

LIEUT. COL. R.A.M.C., T.F.
O.C. 1/2nd HIGHLAND FIELD AMBULANCE

146/2017

1/2nd Highland Field Ambulance.

COMMITTEE FOR THE
MEDICAL HISTORY OF THE WAR
Date   11 MAY 1917

Army Form C. 2118.

WAR DIARY
of
INTELLIGENCE SUMMARY.
(Erase heading not required.)

2nd Highland Field Ambulance B.E.F.

Vol 23. (1).

Vol 2

Place	Date	Hour	Summary of Events and Information	Remarks and references to Appendices
Field	1.3.17		Visited A.D. Station at Anzin. Work on dug-outs and pro- roofing, sandbagging etc of farm yard proceeding satisfactorily. Preparing unit for move to COUCOURT.	SR
	2.3.17		Capt Bruce and 10 men left Haute Avesnes for Coucourt	SR
	3.3.17		Unit moved at 11am from HAUTE-AVESNES to CAUCOURT taking over D.R.S. there from 1/3rd Highland Ambulance and handing over Main Dress. Stn to 1/3rd H.F.Amb. 1/2 an H.F.Amb. still retains A.D. Stn at Anzin and supplies bearers to Lille Road Collecting Post, Madagascar Collecting Post & R.A.P.s.	SR
	4.3.17		Went to ANZIN to inspect work there & on to MADAGASCAR and LILLE ROAD Posts & made fresh arrangements for nursing party. Called at 154th Bde H.Q. and discussed clearing out of ABRI-MOUTON via Brigade Aid Post & then on to ABRI-MOUTON via FANTOME TRENCH. Called on A.D.M.S. on return.	SR

WAR DIARY
INTELLIGENCE SUMMARY
1/2nd High[land] Field Ambulance

Army Form C. 2118.

Vol. 23 (2)

Place	Date	Hour	Summary of Events and Information	Remarks and references to Appendices
Field	5.3.17		To ANZIN, MADAGASCAR, LILLE ROAD, ECURIE, and ROCLINCOURT. Called on A.D.M.S. on return.	S.R.
	6.3.17		To ANZIN, MADAGASCAR, LILLE ROAD and ROCLINCOURT with Captain LUCAS, M.O. i/c 1/8:Arg & Suth'd High'rs to inspect proposed site of 152 Brigade Aid Post. Steering going on in Roclincourt. Work at Anzin and Lille Road progressing steadily.	
	7.3.17		To ANZIN. Saw R.E's about material required.	S.R.
	9.3.17		To ANZIN, LILLE ROAD & ABRI-MOUTON. Work progressing at all places.	S.R.
	10.3.17		Captain 96eighton relieved Captain Browne at A.D.S.	S.R.
			To ANZIN regarding everything such supplies of stength A.D.S. & Aid Posts.	S.R.
	11.3.17		Captain Wallace at A.D.Stn. was relieved by Lieut. Wilson. Relief arranged for 50% for personnel at A.D.S. & Aid Posts. D.M.S. & A.D.M.S. visited D.R.Stn.	S.R.
	12.3.17		To ANZIN, MADAGASCAR and LILLE ROAD with Colonel GRAY, Consulting Surgeon, 1st Army, & Lt. Col. CHILD, R.A.M.C. Permanent h.	S.R.

WAR DIARY
of
INTELLIGENCE SUMMARY.

Army Form C. 2118.

Vol. 23 (3)

Place	Date	Hour	Summary of Events and Information	Remarks and references to Appendices
Field	13.3.17		No medical Operation Orders received.	D.R.
	14.3.17		To ANZIN and 16th Bde H.Qrs regarding hastening of work at Adv: Wouton Entrance. there regime further deepening & some feet further timbering. Enquiring on Lieut. W. who was transferred to 34th Division for duty.	D.R.
	17.3.17		Saw S.O.C. 152 Inf. Bde. regarding Aid Post on FISH AVENUE and the necessity of pushing on work.	D.R.
	18.3.17		To ANZIN, ABRI-MOUTON, SABLIERS and LILLE ROAD Post with O.Qm.S.	D.R.
	19.3.17		D.R.S. considerably over-worked chiefly owing to number of scabies cases.	D.R.
	21.3.17		To ANZIN, LILLE ROAD & MADASCAR POSTS with A.P.M. Re hoots for German Prisoners & routes of evacuation. Work at Lille Road progressing well considering rare that has to be taken against drawing fire. Called on A.D.M.S on return. Col. GRAY, Consulting Surgeon, 3rd Army called & discussed	

WAR DIARY

1/2nd N. Midd Cas... VOL. 23 (H.)

INTELLIGENCE SUMMARY.

Army Form C. 2118.

Place	Date	Hour	Summary of Events and Information	Remarks and references to Appendices
Field			Reviewed	
	22.3.17		Some points regarding, special affairs &c in Reg Aid Posts & Adv. Dress Stn.	A.R.
			Captain SQUAIR rejoins RFA 256 Bde & Captain GRANT to bee duty at A.D.S.	A.R.
	23.3.17		To ANZIN and LILLE ROAD POST. C.R.E. with the latter cleared two feet. Arranged to lower shelter 3 feet with aid of jacks, trenching & running sides first & then digging out flooring. Barricade LILLE ROAD and GENIE trench being s/eeed.	A.R.
			1100 Clarets, 200 stretchers & 2000 s/eed dressings with miscellaneous dressings & splints sent up to ANZIN.	A.N.
	24.3.17		Captain BROWNE & Ptes HOY & TOWSE presented with medal ribbons by G.O.C. VIII Corps. at Parade at FREVILLERS. O.Dr.S vacced.	A.N.
	25.3.17		To ANZIN and then with Captain GRANT to inspect progress	

WAR DIARY
or
INTELLIGENCE SUMMARY.

Army Form C. 2118.
VOL. 22. (5.)

1/2nd Highland Field Ambulance

Place	Date	Hour	Summary of Events and Information	Remarks and references to Appendices
Juset			**Progress** 132/Bde Aid Post in FISH. Avenue, ROCLINCOURT Avenue being shelled and especially FLOTIERS Avenue which was badly knocked about. Aid post has 29' head cover, 2 entrances and will be 40' x 8'. Insufficient for possible casualties and will require to be lengthened when Labour available. Captains MEIGHAN & GRANT at A.D.Sn. relieved by Captains WALLACE & BRUCE.	
	26.3.17		To ANZIN re difficulties in procuring R.E. Stores and question of water supply.	J.R.
	27.3.17		To ANZIN re stores required for R.A.P's.	J.R.
	28.3.17		To ANZIN, ABRI-MOUTON, SOBLIERS & LILLE ROAD POST with A.D.M.S. inspecting accommodation available and work done. MADAGASCAR CAR leaving shelled, possibly owing to sign board erected on top of it. Back via MAROEUIL to inspect Aid Post DEHEN.	J.R. J.R. J.R. J.D.

Army Form C. 2118.

VOL 23. (6)

WAR DIARY
of
INTELLIGENCE SUMMARY.
1/2nd Highland Field Ambulance
(Erase heading not required.)

Instructions regarding War Diaries and Intelligence Summaries are contained in F.S. Regs., Part II. and the Staff Manual respectively. Title pages will be prepared in manuscript.

Place	Date	Hour	Summary of Events and Information	Remarks and references to Appendices
Field	29.3.17		Abus. called.	
			Stores & dressings sent to MAROEUIL Aid Post with F.S. Panu. No. 1.	
	30.3.17		Called on Adm. S. and went with him to Haute Avesnes	SR
			to ANZIN we 2 tons of supplies. Back by MAROEUIL	
			Aid Post.	
	31.3.17		Lieut GREEN, 'C.O. & 8 men detailed for duty	
			with No. 142. 6.6. Stn. at Aubigny for 14 M. 17.	
			Weather for month has been on the whole	
			cold & inclement, a fair amount of snow, some	
			occasional bad frosts & much sleet & rain. This, along	
			with enemy's breaking up of trench routes	
			at intervals, has made the bearers work heavy, and	
			the digging operations at LILLE ROAD POST were	
			difficult.	

J. Orvie -
LIEUT. COL., R.A.M.C., T.F.
O.C. 1/2nd HIGHLAND FIELD AMBULANCE

51st Divn

1/2nd Highland F.A.

COMMITTEE FOR THE
MEDICAL HISTORY OF THE WAR
Date −6 JUN. 1917

WAR DIARY
of 1/2nd High'd F. Amb'ce RAMC
INTELLIGENCE SUMMARY

Army Form C. 2118.
Vol 24

Place	Date	Hour	Summary of Events and Information	Remarks and references to Appendices
Field	1/17		Running B.R. Station at CAUCOURT. Lieut Green, 1 N.C.O. and 8 men proceeded to AUBIGNY for temporary duty with #2 C.C.S.	
	6/17		B.R. Sta. at CAUCOURT handed over to 2/1st H.F.Amb. Unit moved to ANZIN ST AUBIN.	
	7/17		O.M. and 3 O.R. owing to ANZIN having been heavily shelled yesterday and this morning with casualties in billets neighbouring to A.O.S. the personnel of MADAGASCAR C.P. and LILLE RD. Post and Bde. Cooks moved into position in afternoon X day instead of Y. Occupancies LILLE RD. Post hasty. This further facilitated the carrying up of stones to these places. Personnel at LILLE RD. Post strengthened roof of C.P. with sevent twenty five sand bedded in earth, of English shelter tones on roof and hidden in earth along with cut nett beams from dug outs to make attracting surface. Night fine with clear moonlight, but fixed. Refused bags.	
	8/4/17	10.0 am	Interviewed O.C. Tramways re trolley lorries & available trucks. ROCLINCOURT to LILLE RD. Post and MADAGASCAR to ANZIN will be the only two available. Informed O.C. Bearers, SABLIERS and O.E.C.P. MADAGASCAR.	
		10.30 am	O/c Bearers, SABLIERS came down to LILLE RD. Post to report that motor ambulance had not waited the dugout adjacent to R.A.P. There are Rat dugouts in CHEMIN CREUX and R. AVENUE and all occupied (communic- ate with R.D. M.S. 1/9 R Scots and 15th Bde. and Let. O.C. Bearers also to hunt about with R.M.Os. (1/9 R Scots and 1/6 Gord. Hrs.) for any vacant dugouts. – Stones being steadily hauled at CAUCOURT by Q.M. S. Gregory in car allotment for front area.	
		12 noon	O.k. of 116 Gord. Hrs	

Lieut. Col., R.A.M.C., T.F.
O.G. 1/2nd HIGHLAND FIELD AMBULANCE

Army Form C. 2118.

Vol 24 (2)

WAR DIARY or INTELLIGENCE SUMMARY

8/1/2nd H.F. Amb. R.A.M.C.

(Erase heading not required.)

Place	Date	Hour	Summary of Events and Information	Remarks and references to Appendices
Field	8/11	12 noon	Pte. 08/16 Gord Hrs. shell shock delusional insanity, passed on to ANZIN by Gord. Hrs. who brought him in. Had seen no M.O. Shrapnel Bric on C.P.; meat probably for trolley line	
		2pm	O.C. Ganes, FISH AVE. and ROCLINCOURT for 80 personnel. arranged charge in to Batty of British helmets, gauge and nose dressings from London and Chevalier arrived and went distributor to ABRI MOUTON. SAPPERS and FISH AVE Reserve at LILLE RD. Post and ANZIN. General attack moment. Hardly expected them in time.	
		9.30 pm	Capt Dempster called from ABRI MOUTON and one O.C. Hy T.M.B was to fire him only 25 men instead of 50. Report to R.D.M.S. Pte Cauley of Helford who arrived. Had received no notice of this. 3 Gas shells known into ANZIN in afternoon and evening. Gaskells on _____ No casualties. Two Red Cross Stores mentioned above and evac Chevalier return for one at R.A. Personnel from Carlin Barres also g/f from Elgin. Weather fine and sunny all day, but trenches very heavy/wet. Report repairing car from QMS Gregory. HAUTES AVESNES 5. Motor cyclist arrived	
		11 pm	Car up and cleared last cases	
		12 mid night	Car up removed final cases that had come in	
	9/11	2.45 am	LILLE ROAD Post - all hands round - place cleared up	
		4.30 am	Car up	
		5 am		
		5.30 am	Barrage began Walking wounded commenced to come	

O.O. 1/2nd HIGHLAND FIELD AMBULANCE
LIEUT. COL., R.A.M.C., T.F.

Army Form C. 2118.
Vol 24 (3)

WAR DIARY
or ~~Intelligence~~ SUMMARY.

Instructions regarding War Diaries and Intelligence Summaries are contained in F. S. Regs. Part II. and the Staff Manual respectively. Title pages will be prepared in manuscript.

Place	Date	Hour	Summary of Events and Information	Remarks and references to Appendices
Zuid	9/5/17	5.30 am	Nil	
		6 am	Styles commenced working from early cases kit in assembly trenches	
			Weather broken during rain commenced 5.30.	
		6.45 am	O.C. Bearers ABRI MOUTON reports in person numerous Rest arrived the Has 30 of his own Bearers and 25 Heavy T.M.B. Sick to send orderly him to wait for orders. Stretchers bare in this way as well as S.B.C.P. Meanwhile they are using small elements for Stab bearers begin from elsewhere.	
		8.10 am	O.C.P. MADAGASCAR reports 24 German Prisoners available. No demands yet for extra bearers from line. To hold them meanwhile. Cases commencing to come in quickly.	
		8.30 am	O.C. Bearers SABLIERS reports things going on steadily there. Cases now nearly nil — Sent.	
		8.45 am	Some wounded stores going through. Went so far light.	
		8.50 am	SABLIÉ R.S. reports things going quietly and steadily. ABRI MOUTON only a few cases in.	
		10.30 am	Saw Tramway Officer and late notified O.C. FISH AVE. that 6 trolleys are here for was from ROCLINCOURT to LILLE RD. C.P. these are not sufficient. Wire BONT ASK'N. Court so the track runs until to LILLE RD. and traffic ammunition etc. going to ROCLINCOURT entails O.K. and running trolley off the line. All reports show evacuation going on steadily and rapidly considering the distance that has to be covered by the bearers carrying.	
		11 am	O.C. Bearers SABLIERS reports wire Charges Signals from Blue to M.O. Blue that "Butchers" and Bearers are urgently required by No.1 Company between front line and Black line. O.C. SABLIERS also attaches memo from M.O. ½ ¼ R. Scots at same effect and has been sent Bde HQ who estimated 80 cases. Ordered O.C. ABRI MOUTON to send T. N.B. officer	

Army Form C. 2118.

Vol 24(4)

WAR DIARY
of 1/2nd High F. Amb.
INTELLIGENCE SUMMARY.
Rank T.F.

(Erase heading not required.)

Instructions regarding War Diaries and Intelligence Summaries are contained in F. S. Regs., Part II. and the Staff Manual respectively. Title pages will be prepared in manuscript.

Stamp: O.C. 1/2nd HIGHLAND FIELD AMBULANCE
LIEUT. COL., R.A.M.C., T.F.
Signed: Bessie(?)

Place	Date	Hour	Summary of Events and Information	Remarks and references to Appendices
Ecoust	9/1/17	11 am	Officer and 36 men to O.C. SADLIERS. Called with reserve ambulance 5/3 N.F.Amb. ANZIN and sent message to the C.P. MADAGASCAR to bed up 30 stores if required. Also reed message from ABRI MORTON that officer blown to pieces, asking for examination of him, as blood was brought back? ANZIN, also remains coming in.	
		11.15 am	Cleaned 16 cases. Stretcher bearers coming. Message from O.C. FISH AVE. Bearers wanting 3bomen to report to him at FISH AVE. sending message from O.C. SADLIERS that he is to patrol field.	
		1 pm.	No reason given. Men will need to hr. June. Phone DADDS. By 1/8 A.T.S. Mts. Ammunition Dump blown regarding evacuation in afternoon from SADLIERS FISH AVE. All showing more going on steadily.	
		3 pm.	Notified ANZIN to keep all available bearers to LILLE ROAD C.P. Went round SADLIERS and FISH AVE. R.P.s. and our area in front of Bearers and at the same time of Bell Inf. and our Brigadier.	
		4 pm.	ROCLINCOURT came back by trolley line. Called at OS of Bell Inf. to report. R Mts. 1/4 R. Hrs Rie and first 2 new from min, without day light avail. Saw O.C. 1/4 R. Hrs Rie and made best use of phoned 153 Bde. O.C. SADLIERS to assist O.C. Bearers there and men in reserve General all, as the weather is very cold and threatening snow R.M.O. 1/4 Lond. Hrs and 1/6 R. Medical Operations (we cleaning Saulx Field) for parties from Bns in reserve General 153rd referred walks to G., but parties of 50 each to men Butchers and 3 from Nightys. started work in evening, being filled with orders for the purpose, parties to work SADLIERS and FISH AVE. applies received for the purpose. Capt. MOULTON Coy 2 for Stretcher transferred all Capt. Dempster bearers and R.M.O. 1/4th Bn Lord, all night to FISH AVE sundry bearers and needing. Called on Brigadier bearers to Capt. Pillans. at FISH AVE., who all unhurt. Mrs and 1/8 A.T.S Mts., Saw trident. Said he was satisfied from his own knowledge that our work was 152 Bde. going steadily. Capt. Dempster arrived from FISH AVE reports all going strong to-day night	

A 5834   Wt. W4973/M687 750,000 8/16 D. D. & L. Ltd. Forms/C.2118/13.

WAR DIARY
INTELLIGENCE SUMMARY.

Army Form C. 2118.
Vol 24/51

1/2nd High. F. Amb.
Rams. E.F.

Place	Date	Hour	Summary of Events and Information	Remarks and references to Appendices
Field	9/11	4 pm	right and assist him.	
		8 pm	On arriving there found A.D.M.S. but could not get through. Finally a/c C.P. got acutely congested, about time 130 to evacuate, owing to lack of cars. This was largely due to cars being held up by (1) rapidly increasing traffic on all evacuation roads (2) temporary block age of roads by accidents to other motor transport. (3) The shortcut road LILLE ROAD to ANZIN ROAD being now opened by Sappers turned on all German prisoners to evacuate by wheeled trolleys and drawing 4 men to a stretcher to clear Cleared 30 cases in this way and notified ANZIN that at all costs cars must come this way to cases being too bad in other in snow. All such able cases were freely fed with hot soup and tea. And all them blankets employed for extra cover Phoned round A.D.M.S. enquiring re possibility of assistance of M.A.C. cars for ANZIN - HOUDAIN HAVRINC. Later increased number of cars being freed, & the cases were gradually overtaken.	
		11 pm	A.D.M.S. called.	
		12 mid night	Cases lying out being gradually overtaken.	
	10/11	2 am	Majority removed away, snowfalling tonight very cold, approaching frost.	
		5 am	Cases coming in steadily, but in lessening numbers. Large percentage of cases now who are coming from dugouts, shell holes &c. - there who are hit early in the action having field to being silenced. Large proportion of Germans amongst them.	
		9 am	Capt Dempster went to ABRIMOUTON and cabin Rhodesia he had 30 health bearers there ready. Drew C to villace huns as loaders of cars at LILLE ROAD, & huns being stayed out. Sent them to MONGISMONT after feeding.	
		11.30 am	A.D.M.S.	

A.D. 1/2nd HIGHLAND FIELD AMBULANCE
LIEUT. COL. R.A.M.C., T.F.

WAR DIARY / INTELLIGENCE SUMMARY

Army Form C. 2118.

1/2nd Highland Field Ambulance R.A.M.C. T.F.

Vol 34 (6)

Place	Date	Hour	Summary of Events and Information	Remarks and references to Appendices
Field	10/7/17	11.30 am	A.D.M.S. called. Capt Grant called & reported that he had turned his Fontaine and that evacuation was going ahead.	
		noon	A.A. & Q.M.G. Slotherton called. Enquired about evacuation. Satisfied with arrangements &c	
		4 pm	Am R.A.M.C. Various reports from Capts Grant and Pellans to mod reference Stations of Kms attrib R.A.M.C. Each had been reckoning going over forward ahead, as had all M.O.'s in their Bn's R.B. All reported evacuation of wounded as practically complete. Bom's and bh teasing number of wounded coming here and such cars being cars but early in operation — "aftermath" type. Cmd'e detailed report to A.D.M.S. No casualties among bearers during the operation, and all have worked splendidly.	
		6 pm	Capt Pellans called to report after personally visiting H.Q. forward areas again. Conditions found thoroughly satisfactory.	
		8 pm	Cars coming in occasionally only. Practically a a.d.s. Personnel getting a much needed rest.	
		11 pm	Six cars passed through during the night. Snow falling heavily at intervals. News of Capt Blair's death. Sent Car Despatch rider as usual m.o. 1/6/7 R. Hylds.	
		12 noon	Things quiet occasional cars going through several cars of exhaustion and frostbration through the extreme cold, Knighton.	
	11/7	7 am		
		1 pm and 3 pm	Got operation orders re relief here by 2nd Divisional F. Ambce. So the done on 11th Knight 11th/12th. Started checking stores at all hooks. D.A.D.M.S. 2nd Divisional with officers of 5th F. Amb. called D.A.D.M.S. Italia He arranged his ambce up in time by use relief. In confir of him Italy of the R.A.P.s. e turned relieve S.B. Bk 12:15 and Fish Ave, and the R.A.P.s at ANZIN by parties arriving at 9 am pour wounded tomorrow and LILLE RD, C.P. and ANZIN by parties arriving at 9 am pour wounded that this.	

Army Form C. 2118.

WAR DIARY
or
INTELLIGENCE SUMMARY.
(Erase heading not required.)

1/2nd High: F. Ambce.
R.A.M.C. T.F.

Vol 24 (A)(7)

Place	Date	Hour	Summary of Events and Information	Remarks and references to Appendices
Field.	11/9/17	4 pm	that this was reached by A.D.M.S. 51(H) Dn. This will made the first duty of 8th Divisn to get a good and allow relief to be done thoroughly by day light with local guides. Later received sanction of A.D.M.S.	
		6 pm	OC SABLIERS and OC FISH AVE have been sent forward again to make reconnaissance of new ac. changes. Shell holes to have been again for acc. Various new acc reported	
			Body of Capt Blair arrived and sent to MACROON by car in accordance and wishes of OC 1/1 R. Highrs	
		11pm	Things quiet. No attempts nothing.	
	18/9/17	6.30 am	1 officer & 5 O.R's. 2nd Hazard on way to SABLIERS with hands	
			1 " " 100ft " FISH AVE	
		10am	1 " " " arrived with hands to relieve LILLE RD C.P.	
		12 noon	Reliefs complete. all ranks demonstrated to incomers. Receipts signed. Ammunition to M.D.S.	
			Note: Evacuation proceeded steadily from beginning of relief to end. the only delay being the unavoidable and ? ? held up at LILLE RD C.P. owing to road traffic on night 17/18. In any case the ratients were little ? C.P. even though in the open as extra blankets and hot food were available and to a certain extent the congestion was due to food cases up. the evacuation with which cases had been coming down from the front line. It was a combination from the beginning that this want of a road tramway caused into the direct line from delivering artillery and ammunition to reinforce a danger that the road be get the ? ? that acc could be a danger to evacuation. The met this acc ? that had been made to get as much accom. acc at LILLE RD CP as possible, and remaining the time at disposal and that most of the Pioneering was done by R.A.M.C. the accommodation there was	
	13/-/-		Maximum Decreable	

WAR DIARY
INTELLIGENCE SUMMARY

Army Form C. 2118.

Vol 24 (X(8))

O.C. 1/2nd HIGHLAND FIELD AMBULANCE
LIEUT. COL., R.A.M.C., T.F.

Place	Date	Hour	Summary of Events and Information	Remarks and references to Appendices
Gréla	13th 15th		Unit at HQ. On 15th drew 30 Thomas' splints from A Depôt. Fred Stones	
	16/7/17	6 am	Unit moved to ST. NICHOLAS. Taking over R.A.S. there from 28th F. Amb. 9th Div. Sent 700 stretchers up to O/p forward evacuation with 3 horse wagons. 1/30 HQ A/c was obj Zvoolshop and 1 Ford Car running out of Cars. 1 of 3rd HFA. had broken down and gone to works hit.	
		Noon	Major Wellan called and drew a large supply of stores including 10 items as "Splints Cpt Meghan sent up to FAMPOUX. 1 NCO and 30 bearers sent to ST LAURENT BLANGY. Collected old timber and renovated room an afternoon to provide accommodation for patients awaiting treatment that near Ht. T. Amb. Part C be reserved as a mortuary.	
			ADMS called	
	17/4/17	5 pm	Weather wet mud, rail and snow at intervals. Col Grey CB. Consulting Surgeon Third Army with Col. Bruce Canadian from Boss and another officers called. Col Grey ex- pressed himself as highly pleased with the evolution of which. Col Bruce wounded his left the forward areas, many cases of fractures (thighs in Thomas,' upper and fore-arm and leg fractures) having him able to be had exhausted, wrists at A/L further accommodation for being cases before going to Dressing Rooms. A/L Stewart Eure" called. Various advice & dressings sent up. Large number of casualties passed through. Many not on ARRAS- FAMPOUX road.	
	18/4/17	10 am	L'ABBAYETTE Sent up 200 pistols pillows and half of 250 more beds to Alister Asso'c"). Kept 300 pillows here and various more dressings and stabber (from A/L of any finished). Various repair works going on-unsettled weather. A.A. RAMG 84 casualties passed through B/W. 9 hrs and 9 am. called in afternoon Patients & evening Cap. Meghan injured ambu- ance officers have been withdrawn from FAMPOUX with party owing to shelling and R.A.S. having been withdrawn to Stretchd M. village.	
	19/4/17		All 1/2nd HFA. Amb Cars on road the morning deaths cold and wet DMS. Third Army. ADMS. XVII Corps and ADMS 51st H. Div. called DMS in forward	

A.5834 Wt. W4973 M687 750,000 8/16 D.D. & L. Ltd. Forms/C.2118/13.

WAR DIARY
INTELLIGENCE SUMMARY

Army Form C. 2118.

Vol 24 (9) '17

1/2nd High'd F. Amber.
Rame. T.F.

Place	Date	Hour	Summary of Events and Information	Remarks and references to Appendices
Field	19/7/17		Himself in charge of the manner in which cases in front area had been dressed during recent operations, and condition in which they had passed through CCS. Major Tulli called re stores at Brouay. Distribution of bearer personnel and cars in forward area. Such consignment of stretcher pillows arrived from Red Cross Depot at HEM. Finished extra accommodation for cases waiting dressing. Red Cross representative called. Intended for four extra posts, lamps and various stores. Weather better.	
	20/7/17	11am	L'ABBAYETTE. D.A.D.M.S. called and went over various points. Major Tulli down from C.P. at L'ABBAYETTE. Sent up more stores to C.P.	
		2pm	Went up to BLANGY to discuss evacuation of officer with Major Tulli. Evacuation to HAUTES AVESNES very slow owing to traffic. Car leaving here at 8am was not back up to 4pm. Nevertheless plan has never been any undue accumulation of traffic.	
	21/7/17		Fine day. 5 Wolseleys and 2 Fords on road. Enabling two operating cars for putting cases and cleaning room for dressing room overhauled stores. Went to Old Factory to interview A 9 F.J. Amb., who is sending cases in here. Found he had no orders. Communicated with Major Tulli re number of personnel available from his unit for Beau Division and Lent Sub-Division.	
		8pm	2 F.Amb. cars required to left evacuation to M.D.S. owing to Wolseleys BLANGY and L'ABBAYETTE and road between reported pulled off traffic on road all day and numerous casualties brought in at intervals.	
	22/7/17 (V day)		4 Wolseleys and 2 Fords on road. Fine day. Arrangements completed A.D.M.S. called. Called on A.A. & Q.M.G. re extra bearers from F.J. Bearers (100) and T.M.B. (50). First 50 to come here at 9am, second at 10. 3rd at 11am. Each party under an officer, on being fitted with stretchers one to each 2 men to go up by returning empty cars to L'ABBAYETTE. Communicated with Major Tulli who acknowledged D.A.D.M.S. arrived at M.D.S.	
	23/7/17 Z day	12.30am	Reveille	

WAR DIARY
or
INTELLIGENCE SUMMARY.
(Erase heading not required.)

Army Form C. 2118.

Vol 24 (10)

2nd Hghd F Amber
Fame T.F

O.C. 1/2nd HIGHLAND FIELD AMBULANCE
LIEUT. COL., R.A.M.C., T.F.

Place	Date	Hour	Summary of Events and Information	Remarks and references to Appendices
Field	23/4/17 1 day	7am 7.30am	Reveille 5 am Breakfast 5.30am Night Staff relieved at 6 am. Cases coming in.	
		8.30am	Lt Reid brought 3 Amber barons through with "G.S.W. High L". About 30 Shells came over at an entrance.	
		10-11 am	D.T.M.S. called. Several cases from R.N.D. came in. sannied right down from line by stone knockers.	
		11.45 am	Start walk out by night up to Rev A. Reed C.F. Scotch Churches Tent Coffee Bar at "T"NBBAYETTE. Do be in charge of Major Millers.	
	1 pm		All abreast bearers now stationed, viz, 1/5 Bnd Hrs. 2 officers - 81 O.R. 2.M.R.:- 1 officer and 49 O.R. Then had returned for duty at 9, 10 and 11 am and went. Sent up an empty returning cars so as to be spot for want on arrival cases coming in steadily but somewhat slowly owing to traffic or roads. Noticed O/c forward bear: that last bearers had gone.	
	1.30 pm		do	
	4 pm		Evacuation proceeding steadily Ambulance cars busying to M.D.S. slow owing to traffic on ARRAS. St. Pol road.	
	6 pm 10 pm		Evacuation proceeding steadily do	
			Units casualties today :- 6 wounded.	
	24/4/17	8 am	Fine day. Though right time has been a steady stream casualties went out to T. NEBNYETTE to consult with Major Miller regarding times and	
		11 am	situation and withdrawing personnel on relief.	
	4.45 pm		Capt Rees and 13 O.R. of 102 Y. Amb. reported for instruction in clearing forward area. Sent on to Major Miller. Schort. Sgr Major Miller that N° 1658 Pte Sinclair. of this unit was killed in action today.	
	6 pm		102 Y. Amb. of 34th Div. arrived from this Div. Wires he relieved tonight and that his unit be sent by D.A.D.M.S. at 10am. Tomorrow. Weather fine Evacuation proceeding steadily all	

WAR DIARY
of 2nd High'd F. Ambce
INTELLIGENCE SUMMARY. Ramc.T.

Army Form C. 2118.

Vol 24 (19)

Place	Date	Hour	Summary of Events and Information	Remarks and references to Appendices
Field	24/4/17	all day	Unit casualties today:- 1 killed in action 5 wounded.	
	25/4/17	10am	Total patients through A.D.S. pages 5 am 23/4/17 to 5 am. 24/4. handed over to 102 F. Amb. (Lt. Col. Lewin). Weather fine.	
			Notes on Evacuation. In operations of 9th/10th of Apr. 1917 the weather was bad, but bearers from line to Aid Posts went out, went in ROEUX COURT, in hopes to bad Phillips. Chief difficulty in evacuation from C.P. to A.D.S. owing to traffic in rehabitions. 23/4/17 the most the weather was fine and mule day, but the bearers went from line to R.P.S. was exceptionally heavy owing to shell and M.G. fire, while the horse cars from FAMPOUX to FABAYETTE Road especially dangerous were that evacuation to A.D.S. and A.D.S. to M.D.S. while necessary hindered by heavy traffic on road was plenty, owing to St. Aul. cars all working to front and M.A.C. cars being available from A.D.S. to M.D.S. The units casualties in operations of 23/4/24 were all among the bearers viz. 1 killed in action, 2 died of wounds, 3 wounded and returned to duty, 4 evacuated wounded. Total 12.	
	26/4/17	10 am	Unit left ST. NICHOLAS for AGNIÈRES. Billeted in barns. Weather fine.	
	27/4/17		at AGNIÈRES. Weather fine and sunny.	
	28/4/17	10.30 am	Unit moved under orders issued by 152 Bde. to MONTS-EN-TERNOIS by BERLETTE, BERLES, PENIN, MAIZIÈRES, GOUY-EN-TERNOIS. Weather fine and sunny with cold wind. Men billeted in barns.	
	29/4/17		Weather fine and warm. Overhauling Transport, repairing and cleaning G.S. wagons	

WAR DIARY
or
INTELLIGENCE SUMMARY.
(Erase heading not required.)

Army Form C. 2118.

O/C 1/2nd High. F. Amb.
Rams F. Vol 24 (2).

Place	Date	Hour	Summary of Events and Information	Remarks and references to Appendices
Field	29/7/17		G.S. wagons, limbers, and ambulance wagons, sewing fresh clothing to unit, and checking W.E. Capt. Browne to BAILLEUL EN. CORNAILLES to find M.O. 1/7 R. Highrs.	
	30/7/17		At MONTS-EN-TERNOIS. Fine sunny weather. At work on new public latrines for the village as the house was nearly full; cleaning wagons and overhauling equipment.	

Lawrie
LIEUT. COL., R.A.M.C., T.F.
O.C. 1/2nd HIGHLAND FIELD AMBULANCE

B.E.F.

SUMMARY OF MEDICAL WAR DIARIES of

1/2nd Highland Field Ambulance,
    51st Division,
        17th Corps, 3rd Army.

WESTERN FRONT,   APRIL - MAY 1917.

O.C.   Lt.Colonel D. Rorie.

Summarised under the following headings:-

PHASE "B" - BATTLE OF ARRAS.   APRIL - MAY 1917.

1st Period, April 1917. Attack on Vimy Ridge.
2nd Period, May 1917. Capture of Siegfried Line.

B.E.F.

1.

1/2nd High. F.A., 51st Division,　　WESTERN FRONT,
O.C. Lt.Col. D. Rorie.　　APRIL 1917.
17th Corps, 3rd Army.

Phase "B" - Battle of Arras. April - May 1917.
1st Period, April 1917. Attack on Vimy Ridge.

April.　　H.Q. at Caucourt. D.R.S.

6th-7th　　Moves To Anzin St. Aubin on relief at D.R.S. by 2/1st High. F.A.

7th　　Operations Enemy & Moves dets. Owing to Anzin being heavily shelled, with casualties in billets neighbouring to A.D.S., personnel for Madagascar Coll. P. and Lille Rd. P. and Bde. P. moved into position in afternoon of "X" day instead of "Y".

8th　　Operations Enemy & Ops. Enemy Gas. Shrapnel fire on Coll. P. Gas shells in Anzin. No casualties.

9th　　Operations Barrage began 5.30 a.m.

Evacuation Proceeded well throughout day. P.O.W. used at S. Brs.

Parties of 50 each from 1/7th Gord. H. and 1/6th R. High. started clearing battlefield in evening.

At 8 p.m. Coll. P. congested - 130 to evacuate owing to lack of cars. Cars held up by increased traffic on roads, temporary blockage of road by accident, and the short cut road Lille Rd. to Anzin Rd. monopolised by gunners.

All P.O.W. turned out to evacuate by wheeled trolleys and bearing 4 men to a str. to clear. 30 W. cleared in this way.

Later with increased number of cars and clearer roads a normal state was reached.

10th　　At 2 a.m. majority of W. evacuated.

Casualties /

B.E.F.

1/2nd High. F.A., 51st Division,   WESTERN FRONT,
O.C. Lt.Col. D. Rorie.   APRIL 1917.
17th Corps, 3rd Army.

Phase "B", continued.
1st Period, continued.

April.

10th (contd.)   Casualties W. came in steadily. Many who were W. early in action being brought from dugouts, shell holes, etc. By 4 p.m. evacuation practically complete.

12th   Moves To Acq, on relief by 2nd Divn. F.A.

15th   Supplies 50 Thomas splints drawn from "A" depot Med. Stores.

16th   Moves To St. Nicholas.
       Moves det. O & 21 to St. Laurent Blangy.

17th   Casualties Col. Grey, C.B., Consulting Surgeon, 3rd Army, stated "Highly pleased with condition in which W. left forward area. Many cases of fractures (thigh in Thomas's, upper and lower forearm and leg fractures) having been sent to base untouched."

18th   9 p.m. - 9 a.m.   84 W.
       Moves det. & Ops. Enemy. Personnel withdrawn from Fampoux and R.A.P's withdrawn to behind village owing to enemy shelling.

20th   Evacuation Very slow to Haute Avesnes owing to traffic.

21st   5 Wolseleys and 2 Fords on roads.
       2 Fords required to help in evacuation to M.D.S. owing to blockage on road.
       Operations Enemy. Blangy and L'Abbayette and road between shelled.
       Casualties "Numerous."

23rd   Operations Z day.
       Evacuation & Assistance Several W. from R.N.D. received, carried down by P.O.W. All reserve brs. dispatched by 1 p.m. They/

B.E.F.

1/2nd High. F.A., 51st Division,   WESTERN FRONT,
O.C. Lt.Col. D. Rorie.   APRIL 1917.
17th Corps, 3rd Army.

Phase "B", continued.
1st Period, continued.

April.

23rd (contd.)   Evacuation & Assistance (contd.)
They included 2 & 81 1/5th Gord. Hrs. 1 & 49 T.M.B. These were sent by returning empty cars so that men should arrive fresh.

W. came in steadily, but slowly owing to traffic on roads.

Casualties R.A.M.C.   0 & 6 W.

24th   Casualties Steady stream throughout night.
Casualties R.A.M.C. 0 & 1 killed. 0 & 5 W.
Casualties.   Total through A.D.S. from 5 a.m. 23rd
= 747 W.

26th   Moves To Agnieres on relief by 102nd F.A.
Casualties R.A.M.C. Total 23rd/24th
0 & 1 killed, 0 & 2 D. of Wounds. 0 & 9 Wounded.

28th   Moves Under orders of 152nd Bde. moved to Monts-en-Ternois.

B.E.F.

1/2nd High. F.A., 51st Division,   WESTERN FRONT,
O.C. Lt.Col. D. Rorie.   APRIL 1917.
17th Corps, 3rd Army.

Phase "B" - Battle of Arras. April - May 1917.
1st Period, April 1917. Attack on Vimy Ridge.

April.	H.Q. at Caucourt. D.R.S.
6th-7th	Moves To Anzin St. Aubin on relief at D.R.S. by 2/1st High. F.A.
7th	Operations Enemy & Moves dets. Owing to Anzin being heavily shelled, with casualties in billets neighbouring to A.D.S., personnel for Madagascar Coll. P. and Lille Rd. P. and Bde. P. moved into position in afternoon of "X" day instead of "Y".
8th	Operations Enemy & Ops. Enemy Gas. Shrapnel fire on Coll. P. Gas shells in Anzin. No casualties.
9th	Operations Barrage began 5.30 a.m.
	Evacuation Proceeded well throughout day. P.O.W. used at S. Brs.

Parties of 50 each from 1/7th Gord H. and 1/6th R. High. started clearing battlefield in evening.

At 8 p.m. Coll. P. congested - 130 to evacuate owing to lack of cars. Cars held up by increased traffic on roads, temporary blockage of road by accident, and the short cut road Lille Rd. to Anzin Rd. monopolised by gunners.

All P.O.W. turned out to evacuate by wheeled trolleys and bearing 4 men to a str. to clear. 30 W. cleared in this way.

Later with increased number of cars and clearer roads a normal state was reached.

10th   At 2 a.m. majority of W. evacuated.
Casualties

B.E.F.

1/2nd High. F.A., 51st Division,
O.C. Lt.Col. D. Rorie.
17th Corps, 3rd Army.

WESTERN FRONT,
APRIL 1917.

Phase "B", continued.
1st Period, continued.

April.	
10th (contd.)	Casualties W. came in steadily. Many who were W. early in action being brought from dugouts, shell holes, etc. By 4 p.m. evacuation practically complete.
12th	Moves To Acq, on relief by 2nd Divn. F.A.
15th	Supplies 50 Thomas splints drawn from "A" depot Med. Stores.
16th	Moves To St. Nicholas.
	Moves det. O & 21 to St. Laurent Blangy.
17th	Casualties Col. Grey, C.B., Consulting Surgeon, 3rd Army, stated "Highly pleased with condition in which W. left forward area. Many cases of fractures (thigh in Thomas's, upper and lower forearm and leg fractures) having been sent to base untouched."
18th	9 p.m. - 9 a.m. 84 W.
	Moves det. & Ops. Enemy. Personnel withdrawn from Fampoux and R.A.P's withdrawn to behind village owing to enemy shelling.
20th	Evacuation Very slow to Haute Avesnes owing to traffic.
21st	5 Wolseleys and 2 Fords on roads.
	2 Fords required to help in evacuation to M.D.S. owing to blockage on road.
	Operations Enemy. Blangy and L'Abbayette and road between shelled.
	Casualties "Numerous."
23rd	Operations Z day.
	Evacuation & Assistance Several W. from R.N.D. received, carried down by P.O.W. All reserve brs. dispatched by 1 p.m. They/

B.E.F. 3.

1/2nd High. F.A., 51st Division,   WESTERN FRONT,
O.C. Lt.Col. D. Rorie.   APRIL 1917.
17th Corps, 3rd Army.

Phase "B", continued.
1st Period, continued.

April.

23rd (contd.) Evacuation & Assistance (contd.)

They included 2 & 81 1/5th Gord.Hrs. 1 & 49 T.M.B.
These were sent by returning empty cars so that men should arrive fresh.

W. came in steadily, but slowly owing to traffic on roads.

Casualties R.A.M.C.   0 & 6 W.

24th Casualties Steady stream throughout night.
Casualties R.A.M.C. 0 & 1 killed. 0 & 5 W.
~~Casualties R.A.M.C.~~ Total through A.D.S. from 5 a.m. 23rd
= 747 W.

26th Moves To Agnieres on relief by 102nd F.A.

Casualties R.A.M.C. Total 23rd/24th
   0 & 1 killed, 0 & 2 D. of Wounds. 0 & 9 Wounded.

28th Moves Under orders of 152nd Bde. moved to Monts-en-Ternois.

51st Div.

1/2nd Highland F.A.

140/2101

COMMITTEE FOR THE
MEDICAL HISTORY OF THE WAR
Date 10 JUL. 1917

Army Form C. 2118.

WAR DIARY
or
INTELLIGENCE SUMMARY.
(Erase heading not required.)

1/2 Highld Mtd Amb
R.A.M.C. 7

Vol. 25(1)

Place	Date	Hour	Summary of Events and Information	Remarks and references to Appendices
Field	2/5/17		Capt. Thos. S. Stewart reported for duty with unit.	
	3/5/17		Capt. Thos. S. Stewart detailed for temporary duty at 42 C.C. Stn.	
	5/5/17		Lieut. E.A.I. Green returned from leave and detailed same date as M.O. i/c 1st Sea. Highrs.	
			Capt. H.W. Browne, temp. att'd 1/9 R. Highrs, returned to unit for duty.	
	10/5/17		Unit moved from MONTS-EN-TERNOIS to HAUTE-AVESNES and took over unoccupied portion of Main dressing Station there for reception of wounded.	
	13/5/17		Capt. Browne Beaver-Simcoe proceeded to ST. NICHOLAS Advanced Stn. to report to O.C. 2/1 H.F.A.M.B. and to work under his orders. Two Horse Amb. Cars and all Motor Amces (viz. two motorcycles) also sent to report for duty with O.C. 2/1 H.F.A.M.B. at ST. NICHOLAS	
	23/5/17		Capt. A.C. Wallace proceeded on leave to United Kingdom	
	28/5/17		Capt. J. Chalmers reported for duty with unit.	
	29/5/17		Capt. J. Chalmers, posted for duty to 1/7 Gord. Highrs.	
			Capt. R.D. Greer, temp. attached to 1/9 Royal Scots, as M.O.	
			E.S. Melvin, rejoined unit for duty.	

Army Form C. 2118.

WAR DIARY
or
INTELLIGENCE SUMMARY.

1/2 Highld. D. Ambce
R.A.M.C.T.
Vol 25 (II)

(Erase heading not required.)

Place	Date	Hour	Summary of Events and Information	Remarks and references to Appendices
Field	30/5/17		Unit moved from HAUTE AVESNES to TERNAS. No 6464 Corpl Chas Bakewell, & No 1364 Corpl G.M.Lawson awarded Military medals for gallantry displayed between 19th & 25th April 1917. Date of award 17th May '17.	

J.F. Rorie
LIEUT. COL., R.A.M.C., T.F.
O.C. 1/2nd HIGHLAND FIELD AMBULANCE

B.E.F.

SUMMARY OF MEDICAL WAR DIARIES of

1/2nd Highland Field Ambulance,
  51st Division,
    17th Corps, 3rd Army.

WESTERN FRONT, APRIL - MAY 1917.

O.C. Lt.Colonel D. Rorie.

Summarised under the following headings:-

PHASE "B" - BATTLE OF ARRAS. APRIL - MAY 1917.

1st Period, April 1917. Attack on Vimy Ridge.
2nd Period, May 1917. Capture of Siegfried Line.

B.E.F.

1.

<u>1/2nd High. F.A., 51st Division,</u> WESTERN FRONT,
<u>O.C. Lt.Col. D. Rorie.</u> MAY 1917.
<u>17th Corps, 3rd Army.</u>

Phase "B" - Battle of Arras. April - May 1917.
2nd Period, May 1917. Capture of Siegfried Line.

<u>May.</u>	H.Q. at Agnieres.
10th	<u>Moves</u> To Haute Avesnes - took over unoccupied portion of M.D.S.
13th	<u>Moves</u> det. 1 & B.D. to St. Nicholas. A.D.S. under O.C. 2/1st High. F.A.
	<u>Transport</u> 2 Horse Ambs. and all M. Ambs. less 2 Wolseleys, to O.C. 2/1st High. F.A.
14th-29th	<u>Operations</u> R.A.M.C. Routine.
30th	<u>Moves</u> To Ternas.
	<u>Decorations</u> Cpl. Bateman C. and Cpl. Lawson G.M. awarded M.M. for gallantry displayed between 19th-25th April.

B.E.F.

1.

1/2nd High. F.A., 51st Division,

WESTERN FRONT,

O.C. Lt.Col. D. Rorie.

MAY 1917.

17th Corps, 3rd Army.

Phase "B" - Battle of Arras. April - May 1917.

2nd Period, May 1917. Capture of Siegfried Line.

May.	H.Q. at Agnieres.
10th	Moves To Haute Avesnes - took over unoccupied portion of M.D.S.
13th	Moves det. 1 & B.D. to St. Nicholas. A.D.S. under O.C. 2/1st High. F.A.
	Transport 2 Horse Ambs. and all M. Ambs. less 2 Wolseleys, to O.C. 2/1st High. F.A.
14th-29th	Operations R.A.M.C. Routine.
30th	Moves To Ternas.
	Decorations Cpl. Bateman C. and Cpl. Lawson G.M. awarded M.M. for gallantry displayed between 19th-25th April.

140/220

June 1917

S. 1/2nd Highland F.A.

COMMITTEE FOR THE
MEDICAL HISTORY OF THE WAR
Date -7 AUG. 1917

Army Form C. 2118.

WAR DIARY
or
INTELLIGENCE SUMMARY.

1/2nd Highland Field Ambulance
R.A.M.C.

Vol 25 (III)

(Erase heading not required.)

Place	Date	Hour	Summary of Events and Information	Remarks and references to Appendices
Field	1/6/17		Unit resting at TERNAS	
"	4/6/17		Unit moved from TERNAS to CONTEVILLE.	
"	5/6/17		Unit moved from CONTEVILLE to COYECQUE.	
"	6/6/17		Major (temp. Lieut.-Col.) D. Rose. Officer Commanding, awarded Distinguished Service Order for Distinguished Conduct in the Field dated 3rd June 1917.	
"	8/6/17		Unit moved from COYECQUE to St. MARTIN au LAERT.	
"	9/6/17		Unit moved from St. MARTIN au LAERT to EPERLECQUES. Lieut-Colonel D. Rose takes up duty as A.D.M.S. in the absence of Colonel Fleming on leave.	
"	10/6/17		Unit open for admitting patients at 2.0 pm from 152 Infantry Brigade. Divisional Rest Station opened. Captain Browne detailed to hold sick parade at Convalescent Co. daily. Captain Wallace returned from leave.	
"	11/6/17		Captain Bruce detailed to see the sick of Rev. Duffley Col. at WATTEN daily.	
"	13/6/17		Captain Meighan proceeds on leave	
"	14/6/17		Sis Nursing Orderlies detailed for duty with Second Army Musketry School	

A5834 Wt. W4973 M687 750,000 8/16 D. D. & L. Ltd. Forms/C.2118/13.

Army Form C. 2118.

WAR DIARY
of 1/2nd Highland Fd Amb&lance
INTELLIGENCE SUMMARY. R. a. M. C.
Vol 25 (2)

(Erase heading not required.)

Instructions regarding War Diaries and Intelligence Summaries are contained in F. S. Regs., Part II. and the Staff Manual respectively. Title pages will be prepared in manuscript.

Place	Date	Hour	Summary of Events and Information	Remarks and references to Appendices
Hutch	17/6/17		Lieut-Colonel D. Rorie proceeds on leave	
"	18/6/17		Captain McIntosh assumes temporary command. Captain Wallace detailed as M. O. i/c McMostry School in the absence of Captain Low on leave.	
"	19/6/17		Regimental Sports held to day	
"	20/6/17		Captains Browne and Bruce detailed to sit on Medical Board at A. D. M. S. Office Captain Grant detailed for temp. duty at D. D. M. S. XVIII. Corps Office	
"	21/6/17		Unit moved from EPERLECQUES to CLAIRMARIS minus one section which is remaining to receive sick from 1/2nd McMostry School. Hospital open at CLAIRMARIS for Brigade Sick.	
"	25/6/17		Motor Ambulances + water carts carefully overhauled and cleaned	
"	26/6/17		Captain Maughan reported back from leave	
"	28/6/17		Captain Sloan detailed for temp duty at 56 N.A.G.	
"	29/6/17		Lieut-Colonel D. Rorie returned from leave.	
"	30/6/17		Captain Wallace detailed as M. O. i/c of 71st (Army) Field Artillery Brigade.	

D. Rorie
LIEUT. COL. R.A.M.C. T.
O.C. 1/2nd HIGHLAND FIELD AMBULANCE

B.E.F.

SUMMARY OF MEDICAL WAR DIARIES OF 1/2nd Highland F.A.

51st Div.   8th Corps.   5th ARMY.

18th Corps from June 22nd-23rd.

Western Front Operations - June - 1917.

Officer Commanding - Lt.Col. D. Rorie (T).

SUMMARISED UNDER THE FOLLOWING HEADING:-
Phase "D" - Battle of Messines - June - 1917.

B.E.F.

<u>1/2nd Highland F.A. 51st Div. 8th Corps. 5th ARMY.</u>
<u>Officer Commanding - Lt.Col. D. Rorie (T).</u>   WESTERN FRONT.
                                                  June 1917.

<u>18th Corps</u> from 22nd-23rd June.

<u>PHASE "D" - Battle of Messines - June - 1917.</u>

<u>Headquarters at EPERLECQUES.</u>

June 10th.	<u>Medical Arrangements</u>. Unit opened Div. R.S.
17th.	<u>Moves</u>. Detachment. O & 6 to 2nd ARMY Musketry School.
22nd-23rd.	<u>Transfer</u>. To 18th Corps.
	<u>Moves</u>. To CLAIR MARIS less detachment at 2nd ARMY Musketry School.

B.E.F.

1/2nd Highland F.A. 51st Div. 18th Corps. 5th ARMY.

Officer Commanding - Lt.Col. D. Rorie (T).   WESTERN FRONT.
                                              June 1917.

PHASE "D" - Battle of Messines - June - 1917.

Headquarters at EPERLECQUES.

June 22nd-23rd. Transfer. To 18th Corps.

    Moves. To CLAIR MARIS less detachment at 2nd ARMY Musketry School.

B.E.F.

SUMMARY OF MEDICAL WAR DIARIES OF 1/2nd Highland F.A.

51st Div.   8th Corps.   5th ARMY.

18th Corps from June 22nd-23rd.

Western Front Operations - June - 1917.

Officer Commanding - Lt.Col. D. Rorie (T).

SUMMARISED UNDER THE FOLLOWING HEADING:-
Phase "D" - Battle of Messines - June - 1917.

B.E.F.

1/2nd Highland F.A. 51st Div. 18th Corps. 5th ARMY.

Officer Commanding - Lt.Col. D. Rorie (T).   WESTERN FRONT.
June 1917.
18th Corps from 22nd-23rd June 1917.

PHASE "D" - Battle of Messines - June - 1917.

Headquarters at EPERLECQUES.

June 10th.   Medical Arrangements. Unit opened Div. R.S.
17th.   Moves. Detachment. O & 6 to 2nd ARMY Musketry School.
22nd-23rd.   Transfer. To 18th Corps.
             Moves. To CLAIR MARIS less detachment at 2nd ARMY Musketry School.

B.E.F.

18th Corps from 22nd-23rd June.
1/2nd Highland F.A. 51st Div. 8th Corps. 5th ARMY.

Officer Commanding - Lt.Col. D. Rorie (T).   WESTERN FRONT
                                              June 1917.

PHASE "D" - Battle of Messines - June - 1917.

Headquarters at EPERLECQUES.

June 22nd-23rd. Transfer. To 18th Corps.

    Moves. To CLAIR MARIS less detachment at 2nd ARMY
    Musketry School.

1/2nd Highland F.A.

COMMITTEE FOR THE
MEDICAL HISTORY OF THE WAR
Date 10 SEP. 1917

Army Form C. 2118.

VOL. 27 (1)

WAR DIARY of 1/2 Highld 3d Ambce
INTELLIGENCE SUMMARY.
(Erase heading not required.)

Place	Date	Hour	Summary of Events and Information	Remarks and references to Appendices
FIELD	1/3/17 to 23/3/17		Unit engaged in collection of sick from Brigade. Painting, repairing of equipment, repairing pack saddery.	
	2/3/17		Capt S.S. Meghan detailed to report & receive charge of 1/7 R.O.Rifles during absence on leave, of R.M.O.	
	4/3/17		50 O.R. sent to report for duty to O.C., XVIII Corps Main Dressing Station detached section in charge of hospital for sick of It Corps Mechancy. School rejoined unit this date.	
	8/3/17		20 O.R. sent to report to O.C. 1/3 W.A. Ambce for construction work	
	13/3/17		Capt Browne proceeded on leave.	
	15/3/17		Capt Bruce detailed to take duty as temp'y M.O. /o 51 D.A.C.	
	16/3/17		A detachment of Sent Division of Ambce proceeded to XVIII Corps Main Dressing Station for duty there	
			Capt Wallace rejoined unit from 77 (Army) F.A. Ba.	
			Capt Stewart rejoined unit from 56 H.A.G.	
	20/3/17		A party consisting of eight bearers detailed to each of the Battalions of 153 Brigade for duty during forthcoming operations.	
	22/3/17		Horse Transport moved to WORMHOUDT	
	23/3/17		Horse Transport moved from WORMHOUDT to XVIII C.M.D. Sta.	
	24/3/17		Unit less Horse Transport moved from CHAIRMARAIS to XVIII C.M.D. Sta.	

Army Form C. 2118.

WAR DIARY 1/2 Highland Ambce
of
INTELLIGENCE SUMMARY.
(Erase heading not required.)

Vol. 27 (2)

Instructions regarding War Diaries and Intelligence Summaries are contained in F. S. Regs., Part II. and the Staff Manual respectively. Title pages will be prepared in manuscript.

Place	Date	Hour	Summary of Events and Information	Remarks and references to Appendices
FIELD	28/1/17		3 Ambce Cars of 33rd Fd Ambce working A.D.S. ESSEX FARM relieved by similar number from this unit.	
	29/1/17 30/1/17 30/1/17		Capt Browne returned from leave. Ambce reinforced unit from 57 A.C.R.b.	
			Bearers already detached (34 O.R.) under charge of Capt Melvin and Capt Steven proceeded to front area for duty.	
	29/1/17		XVIII Corps O.S.U. opened for wounded at 12 noon	

B. Rorrie
LIEUT. COL. R.A.M.C. T.F.
O.C. 1/2nd HIGHLAND FIELD AMBULANCE

B.E.F.

SUMMARY OF MEDICAL WAR DIARIES OF 1/2nd Highland F.A.
51st Div. 18th Corps. 5th ARMY.

Western Front Operations - July - 1917.

Officer Commanding - Lt.Col. D. Rorie (T).

SUMMARISED UNDER THE FOLLOWING HEADINGS :-
Phase "D" 1. Passchendaele Operations, "July-Nov. 1917".

(a) Operations commencing 1/7/17.

(b) Operations commencing 1/10/17.
Canadians attacked Passchendaele, Oct 30th.
Canadians took Passenchendaele, Nov, 6th.

B.E.F.

1/2nd Highland F.A. 51st Div. 18th Corps.   5th ARMY. WESTERN FRONT.
Officer Commanding - Lt.Col. D. Rorie (T).   July 1917.

PHASE "D" 1. Passchendaele Operations, July-Nov. 1917.
    (a) - Operations commencing 1/7/17.

Headquarters at CLAIRMARIS.

July 4th.   Moves. Detachment. O & 50 to 18th Corps M.D.S.
            Detachment at 2nd ARMY Musketry School rejoined Headquarters.

8th.   O & 20 to O.C. 1/3rd Highland Field Ambulance for constructional work.

16th.   Detachment of T.D. to 18th Corps M.D.S.

22nd.   Moves. Detachment.) 8 bearers to each Battalion of
    Medical Arrangements.)
153rd Infantry Brigade for duty during forthcoming operations.

24th.   Moves. To 18th Corps M.D.S.

28th.   Moves. Transport.) 3 Amb. cars of 33rd F.A. working
    Medical Arrangements.)
    A.D.S. Essex Farm relieved by similar number from unit.

29th.   Medical Arrangements. 18th Corps M.D.S. opened for reception of wounded at 12 noon.

30th.   Moves. Detachment.) 2 & 34 bearers to front area for duty.
    Medical Arrangements.)

B.E.F.

SUMMARY OF MEDICAL WAR DIARIES OF 1/2nd Highland F.A.

51st Div. 18th Corps. 5th ARMY.

Western Front Operations - July - 1917.

Officer Commanding - Lt.Col. D. Rorie (T).

SUMMARISED UNDER THE FOLLOWING HEADINGS :-
Phase "D" 1. Passchendaele Operations, "July-Nov. 1917".

(a) Operations commencing 1/7/17.

(b) Operations commencing 1/10/17.
Canadians attacked Passchendaele, Oct 30th.
Canadians took Passenchendaele, Nov, 6th.

B.E.F.

1/2nd Highland F.A. 51st Div. 18th Corps.   5th ARMY. WESTERN
                                                      FRONT.
Officer Commanding - Lt.Col. D. Rorie (T).   July 1917.

PHASE "D" 1. Passchendaele Operations, July-Nov. 1917.
       (a) - Operations commencing 1/7/17.

Headquarters at CLAIRMARIS.

July 4th.   Moves. Detachment. O & 50 to 18th Corps M.D.S.
                          Detachment at 2nd ARMY Musketry School
             rejoined Headquarters.

8th.   O & 20 to O.C. 1/3rd Highland Field
             Ambulance for constructional work.

16th.   Detachment of T.D. to 18th Corps M.D.S.

22nd.   Moves. Detachment.) 8 bearers to each Battalion of
             Medical Arrangements.)
             153rd Infantry Brigade for duty during forthcoming
             operations.

24th.   Moves. To 18th Corps M.D.S.

28th.   Moves. Transport.   ) 3 Amb. cars of 33rd F.A. working
             Medical Arrangements.)
                          A.D.S. Essex Farm relieved by
             similar number from unit.

29th.   Medical Arrangements. 18th Corps M.D.S. opened for reception of
             of wounded at 12 noon.

30th.   Moves. Detachment.) 2 & 34 bearers to front area for duty.
             Medical Arrangements.)

1st Highland F.A.

COMMITTEE FOR THE
MEDICAL HISTORY OF THE WAR
Date -1 OCT. 1917

WAR DIARY or INTELLIGENCE SUMMARY

Army Form C. 2118.

1/1st Highland Field Ambulance

Vol 28 (1)

Place	Date	Hour	Summary of Events and Information	Remarks and references to Appendices
FIELD	1/8/17		Tent division engaged at XVIII C.M.O.L. Stn. A.23.C.2.9 Sheet 28 along with Tent division of 134 F.A. A.N.B. Bearer division working in forwarding area.	
	2/8/17		Capt. St. Browne detailed to take medical charge of RFA 256 Bde in relief of Lieut. Dickey.	
	4/8/17		Capt. Meghan detached to take medical charge of RFA 258 Bde in relief of Capt. Spiers.	
	6/8/17		Capt. Wallace detailed to report to Col. R.E. 51 Divn. in relief of Capt. Greer on leave.	
	8/8/17		Two Tent Sub-divisions relieved by Two Tent Sub-divisions of 11th Divn. Moved from Main Dressing Station to St. Jansbeter Begaen. Lt. Col. Rose D.S.O. appointed A.D.S. XVIII Corps Main Dressing Station area near rail halt. Capt. Malcolm Tent Sub. Division. Bearer Division moved back independently. Tent & new dressing of unit at St. Jansbeter Begaen. Unit opens hospital for reception of sick who are likely to recover in	
	9/8/17		72 hours.	
	11/8/17		Capt. Bruce proceeded on leave.	
	17/8/17		Capt. Skeen detailed to report for duty to O.C. No. 93 Labour Group. Unit is struck off strength of unit.	
	19/8/17		Capt. Inance reported temp. for duty from 371 H.F.A.M.S.	
	21/8/17		Capt. Greer returned from leave.	
	26/8/17		Capt. Meghan evacuated wounded.	

Army Form C. 2118.

WAR DIARY 1/9 High Dr Amor
—of—
INTELLIGENCE SUMMARY.
Vol 28 (2)

(Erase heading not required.)

Place	Date	Hour	Summary of Events and Information	Remarks and references to Appendices
Seed	26/5/17		Capt Torrance reported to 3/1 Dr Amos for duty	
	27/5/17		Capt Gillespie RAMC reported for duty	
	29/5/17		Unit moved to XVIII Corps Main Dressing Station in relief of two sections of 1/1st Wessex Fd Amb. Lieut. Young NZ reported for duty	

J. Rorie
Lt Col.
O.C. 1/2 HFA.

140/24 38.

1/2nd Highland. F.A.

Sept. 1917

COMMITTEE FOR THE
MEDICAL HISTORY OF THE WAR
Date -5 NOV. 1917

WAR DIARY 1/7 Highd Fd Amce
INTELLIGENCE SUMMARY
Army Form C. 2118.

Vol 29 (1)

Place	Date	Hour	Summary of Events and Information	Remarks and references to Appendices
FIELD	1/9/17		Bearers to proceed to front area report to O.C. 3t H.F.A.M.S	
	9/9/17		2nd division engaged at XVIII C.M.D.S. A.23.c.2.9 Sheet 28.	
	12/9/17		Capt Bruce detailed to 1/7 Gordon Highrs in relief of Capt Buchanan as M.O. i/c.	
	13/9/17		Capt Melvin proceeded on leave to United Kingdom	
	27/9/17		Capt Melvin returned from leave.	
	13/9/17		16 Bearers to proceed to Seay farm report to O/c there.	
	19/9/17		Solde Rouge hands over charge of XVIII C.M.D.She to O.C. 34 Fd Amce	
	24/9/17		2nd division relieved by 2nd Division of 11 Division and moved to Seigo Camp.	
			Bearer Division moved from forward area to Seigo Camp Joined remainder of unit there.	
			Capt Browne rejoined unit from 255 Bde. R.F.A.	
			Capt Frank struck off strength of unit on being posted to 62 C.C.She.	
			Q.M. & Hon Lieut Johnstone R.G. reported from 134 Fd Ams for duty	
			Lieut V.A. Young, U.S.M.C. detailed for duty with 255 Bde R.F.A. vice	
			Capt Browne.	
	26/9/17		Capt Wallace proceeded to new area in charge of Billeting Party	

Army Form C. 2118.

WAR DIARY
INTELLIGENCE SUMMARY.

(Erase heading not required.)

1/3 Highland Fd Ambce

Vol 29 (2)

Place	Date	Hour	Summary of Events and Information	Remarks and references to Appendices
Field	29/9/17		The unit moved to new area. General Transport proceeding to Brower for entraining.	
	30/9/17		Motor Transport moved by road to Achiet le Grand. The unit entrained at Brower moved to Achiet le Grand area arriving on morning of 1st Oct.	

N. Milne
Capt. R.A.M.C. (T.F.)
o/c 1/3 nd H.F. Amb.

20 OCT 1917

Hort Highland F.A.

140/2/99

6/8/1917

COMMITTEE FOR THE
MEDICAL HISTORY OF THE WAR
Date — 8 DEC. 1917

WAR DIARY

Army Form C. 2118.

of 1/2nd Highland Fd. Ambulance

Vol 30 (1)

INTELLIGENCE SUMMARY

(Erase heading not required.)

Place	Date	Hour	Summary of Events and Information	Remarks and references to Appendices
Field	3/9		A party of one officer and 26 other ranks proceeded to Bopry-Becquerelle for relief of R.A.P.'s and Relay Posts on Divisional Front. Another party of one officer and 26 other ranks proceeded to take over the Advanced Dressing Station at Henin and Harlure.	
	4/10/17		Parties of 30 other ranks reported from each of the 1/3rd and 2/1st Highland Field Ambulances.	
	5/10/17		50 other ranks proceeded to complete relief of R.A.P.'s and A.D.O.'s and to form reserve of bearers at Henin and Harlure.	
			Remainder of unit proceeded to new Headquarters Bovry Becquerelle.	
	5/10/17		Lieut W.F. Williams, M.S.R. reported for duty.	
	6/10		18 Other ranks were detailed as a working party for 181/Tunnelling Co. R.E.	
	8/10/17		Lieut W.F. Williams relieved Capt. Bruce as O/C 1/4 Gordon Hghrs.	
	10/10/17		Captain Bruce rejoined unit for duty.	
	13/10/17		Captain McElvor detailed to act as O/C 1/5 Gordon Hghrs.	
	13/10/17		Captain Britton proceeded on leave to United Kingdom.	
	14/10/17		Lieut Denny M.D. M.C. rejoined unit from the Royal Hghrs and relieved Captain McElvor as O/C 1/5 Gordon Hghrs.	
	15/10/17		Captain McElvor rejoined unit for duty.	
			Lieut Johnston proceeded on leave to United Kingdom.	

Army Form C. 2118.

WAR DIARY
or of 1/2nd Highland Fd Ambulance.
INTELLIGENCE SUMMARY.
(Erase heading not required.)

(Vol 30 (11))

Instructions regarding War Diaries and Intelligence Summaries are contained in F. S. Regs., Part II. and the Staff Manual respectively. Title pages will be prepared in manuscript.

Place	Date	Hour	Summary of Events and Information	Remarks and references to Appendices
Field	19/9/17		2 N.C.O.s and three men awarded Military Medal for gallantry displayed in the field between 19th and 25th September 1917.	
	29/10/17		Major J. J. MacIntosh reported for duty.	
	31/9/17		Unit moved from Doiry Bacquerelle to Montonecourt.	

J MacIntosh Major
Lieut-Col. R.A.M.C., T.F.
O.C. 1/2nd HIGHLAND FIELD AMBULANCE

40/2578

1/2nd Highland F.A.

COMMITTEE FOR THE
MEDICAL HISTORY OF THE WAR
Date   17 JAN.1918

Army Form C. 2118

WAR DIARY
or
INTELLIGENCE SUMMARY.

(Erase heading not required.)

1/2nd Highland Field Ambulance 2nd Camb.(T)

Place	Date	Hour	Summary of Events and Information	Remarks and references to Appendices
MONTENESCOURT	1/11/17		In rest area, collecting Brigade sick, hospital for retaining slight sick cases for 48 hours. Checking Equipment &c.	
	5/11/17		Party of 50. O.R. sent to DAINEVILLE for Agricultural work.	
	13/11/17		Anniversary of Battle of BEAUMONT HAMEL celebrated. General Holiday — Sports dinner and concert	
	3/11/17		Captain S.S. MEIGHAN reported for duty.	
	1/11/17		Lt. Col. D. RORIE on leave to U.K. 1.11.17 – 1.12.17.	
			MAJOR J.F. MACINTOSH assumes command.	
	6/11/17		Captain S.S. MEIGHAN on leave to U.K. 6.11.17 – 21.11.17.	
	15/11/17		2 Officers and 50 other Ranks proceeded to IV. Corps Area for duty at an A.D.Station in Havrincourt Wood.	
	16/11/17		Transport left MONTENESCOURT by road for 2 days march route to ROCQUIGNY.	
	17/11/17		Dismounted personnel by rail march route to ROCQUIGNY.	

Army, Form C. 2118.

WAR DIARY
or
INTELLIGENCE SUMMARY.

(Erase heading not required.) 1/2nd Highland Field Ambulance T.F.

Vol. 31. (")

Place	Date	Hour	Summary of Events and Information	Remarks and references to Appendices
Field.	18/11/17		Unit moved to A.D.Station in Havrincourt Wood-Sheet 57½c - Q.M.d.1.8. Horse Transport to NEUVILLE BOURJONVAL and Mechanical Transport to RUYAULCOURT.	
	19/11/17		Preparing for active operations. Relieving from 1/3 & 7/1 st H.T ambulances reported at 6.0pm. Bearers from Infantry & T.M.B'tys also reported at 6.0pm.	
	20/11/17		First of wounded arriving about 10.0am & evacuation proceeded smoothly throughout the day by Decauville Railway and ambulance cars. During the day over 500 cases were evacuated, 25% being German. About 6.0pm a party took over R.A.P. at TRESCAULT & formed a new Adv. Dressing Station, evacuating then being by car to E.C.S. and to canteen tent at Q.M.d.1.8 (Sheet 57c) for transfer by Decauville Railway & thence to E.C. Stn & main Dressing Station. Transport moved from NEUVILLE BOURJONVAL to Q.M.d.1.8.	

A5834 Wt.W4973 M687 750,000 8/16 D.D.& L.Ltd. Forms/C2118/13.

WAR DIARY
INTELLIGENCE SUMMARY

Army Form C. 2118.

Vol. 31. (III.)

/2nd Highland Field Ambulance Ramb.(T.)

Place	Date	Hour	Summary of Events and Information	Remarks and references to Appendices
Fins	21/11		Evacuation still proceeding satisfactorily as on evening of 20 S. Site for new A.D.S. taken at FLESQUIERES & in afternoon of 21st all details including transport proceeded to the new Bowing 15yt & 3 men at A.M.D.1.8 to evacuate stragglers owing to A.D.S. all went weste mtie unit arrived at Nene Crater on TRESCAULT - RIBECOURT road when it was found further that it was impossible for transport to proceed further. Dismounted personnel however has kept on and opened A.D.S. at RIBECOURT and at FLESQUIERES, taking as much stores as possible by wheeled stretchers & hand cars of evacuating cases by same means to Nine Crater when they were met by Divisional Ambulance cars & evacuated to TRESCAULT & thence to C.C. Stn by M.A.C. At this moment actually from A.D.Stns were being run by the unit, viz. FLESQUIERES, TRESCAULT and A.M.D.1.8 in addition to the loading point at RIBECOURT, Stones had to be carried at Nine Crater where all patients landed from a considerable distance	

WAR DIARY
INTELLIGENCE SUMMARY

Army Form C. 2118.

2nd H.F. [Field Ambulance] Vol. 31. (iv.)

Place	Date	Hour	Summary of Events and Information	Remarks and references to Appendices
Field	22/11		Late last night transport were parked near Mine Crater & wagons half unloaded & during morning moved up to FLESQUIERES — (at Lorre to each wagon) returning for second half of load. The first wagons taken out were the 3 horse ambulance wagons eighty loaded with stretchers, blankets and dressings & with 1 horse to each wagon. They left the Mine Crater about 2-0am & arrived at FLESQUIERES about 3-30am. From this time to about 10-0am evacuation was carried on the same as during the night, but for this stone ambulance wagons took the road & assisted in the evacuation from R.A.P's to Mine Crater. Early in the afternoon they were reinforced by 6 horse ambulance wagons from 1/3 wt & 2/1st H.F. Ambulance which brought up sufficient blankets & stretchers to carry on. From this moment evacuation went on smoothly except for the fact that large motor ambulances failed to get forward.	

A5834 Wt.W4973 M687 750,000 8/16 D.D. & L. Ltd. Forms/C.2118/13.

WAR DIARY
of
2nd Highland (Erase heading not required.) Ambulance Corps (r)

INTELLIGENCE SUMMARY.

Army Form C. 2118.

Vol. 31 (r)

Place	Date	Hour	Summary of Events and Information	Remarks and references to Appendices
Field	22/11		About 2.0 am Captain R.T. BRUCE & Padre A. GRANT were reported taken prisoners by the enemy during an enemy counter attack on the village of FONTAINE-notre-DAME.	
	23/11		Evacuation still proceeding mostly & continuing to do so throughout the day. In the evening large ambulance cars managed to reach FLESQUIERES via MARCOING, but could only make one run as it took them 4 hours to run to C.C.S. They only returned about 6.0 am on 24th. During night 23/24 orders were received to entrain at YPRES on 24th & that ambulance of Guards Division would be relieved by Ambulance early in the morning.	
	24/11		Relief was duly completed & dismounted personnel entrained at YPRES at 11-30 am. Transport travelled by road to MILLENCOURT.	

James Bar

Army Form C. 2118.

Vol. 31 (vi)

WAR DIARY
INTELLIGENCE SUMMARY.

(Erase heading not required.)

1/2nd H.T Ambulance Ramc (T.)

Place	Date	Hour	Summary of Events and Information	Remarks and references to Appendices
Field	25.11.17		Dismounted Reserve detrained at AVELUY & proceeded by march route to bivouacs in MILLENCOURT, arriving about 4.0 a.m.	
	26/28/11		Transport arrived about 5. a.m. Hospital for Brigade sick opened. Checking equipment &c.	

J.S. McCulloch Major
temp. O.C. 1/2nd HIGHLAND FIELD AMBULANCE

1st Highland F.A.

COMMITTEE FOR THE
MEDICAL HISTORY OF THE WAR
Date −1 FEB. 1918

Army Form C. 2118.

WAR DIARY
or
INTELLIGENCE SUMMARY.
(Erase heading not required.)

Vol. 32 (1)

Place	Date	Hour	Summary of Events and Information	Remarks and references to Appendices
Field	1.12.17		Unit moved from Millencourt, 30.11.17, arriving O.16.d. at 8 am 1.12.17. Captain James Sutton Brummure, M.O., R.C., U.S.A., reported for duty.	
	2.12.17		2 Officers and 12 Other Ranks, carrying 2 days rations, reported to O.C. Bearers, 2/3rd London Field Ambulance, DOIGNIES. 2 Officers and 40 Other Ranks, carrying do Lieut. Col. W. Rorie rejoined unit after month's leave.	
	3.12.17		Unit moved to BEUGNY, 11 N.C.Os and 20 men reported to O.C., forward evacuation (Lieut. Col. W. Rorie, N.S.O.) at DOIGNIES.	
	6.12.17		39 Other Ranks, 1/2 High. Field Ambce., 16 Other Ranks 1/3 do. do. Y. Ambce., 21 other Ranks 2/1 High. Field Ambd. relieved from line on the night of the 5th and held in reserve at 1/2 Highland Field Ambulance Headquarters. Captain A.C. Mallace rejoined unit from 1/6 Gordon Highrs.	
	11.12.17		One man A.S.C. M.T. attd awarded Bar to Military Medal, One M.C.O. + one man, A.S.C. M.T. attd and One man A.S.C. do. Y. attd, awarded Military Medal. DOIGNIES	
	14.12.17		Captain G.S. Milwin relieved Captain S.S. Meighan at Advanced Dressing Station, DOIGNIES	
	16.12.17		Major D.F. MacIntosh and 3 other ranks proceeded to 51st (HIGH) Divnl. Rest Camp.	
	17.12.17		Captain J.S. Brummette relieved Lieut. Denning as Bearer Factory, Advanced Dressing Station. Lieut. Fleming attached to report to O.C. 1/5 Seaforth Highrs.	
	23.12.17		Lieut. Shatner reported for duty with this Ambulance from O.O. 1/5 Seaforth Highrs.	
	28.12.17		Lieut. Col. W. Rorie takes duty as of A.D.m.S. 51st (High) Division. Captain S.W. Milwin rejoined Unit from A.D.m.S.	

WAR DIARY
or
INTELLIGENCE SUMMARY.

(Erase heading not required.)

Army Form C. 2118.

Vol 32 (2)

Place	Date	Hour	Summary of Events and Information	Remarks and references to Appendices
FIELD.	24.12.17		Captain S.S. Meighan proceeded to advance Dressing Station, Doignies.	
	26.12.17		Captain R.Y. Bruce reported as Prisoner of War in Germany.	
	27.12.17		Lieut Shannon relieved Captain Martin Smith, 1/3 H.F. Ambce at advanced Dressing Station.	
	31.12.17		Captain S.S. Meighan mentioned in Sir Douglas Haig's Despatch of 17th November 1917 (London Gazette 24.12.17)	

Spencer Bolais
CAPTAIN
R.A.M.C. (T)
1/2 HIGHLAND FIELD AMBCE.

[Stamp: 1/2nd HIGHLAND FIELD AMBULANCE 31 DEC 1917 R.A.M.C. (T) B.E.F.]

12nd Highland F.A.

COMMITTEE FOR
MEDICAL HISTORY OF ...
Date -4 MAR 1918

SECRET.

WAR DIARY
of
INTELLIGENCE-SUMMARY.

1/2nd Highland Field Ambulance, R.A.M.C., T.F.

Vol. 33 (1)

Army Form

Place	Date	Hour	Summary of Events and Information	Remarks and references to Appendices
BEUGNY.	1-1-18.		Unit carrying on with evacuation from line as taken over on 3/12/17 assisted by bearers of 1/3rd and 2/1st H.F.Ambulances. Captain H.W. Browne returned from leave.	
	4-1-18.		Tent-sub division sent to report for temporary duty with No. 29 C.C.Stn. at GREVILLERS.	
	5-1-18.		Captain Brummette, M.O.R.C., U.S.A. reported for duty on relief from A.D.S., Beetroot Factory.	
	10-1-18.		Captain Brummette proceeded to Boulogne for duty under D.D.M.S. there.	
	10-1-18.		Captain W.B. Ray and Lieut. E.W. Fiske, U.S.Army reported for instructional purposes.	
	13-1-18.		Advance party consisting of 2 N.C.O's and 15 men sent to new area. (Achiet-le-Grand to prepare billets for unit.	
	17-1-18.		Captain W.B.Ray and Lieut. E.W. Fiske, U.S.Army returned to Base Hospital No. 27 on completion of course of instruction.	
	18-1-18.		Major George Waterston Miller, D.S.O., R.A.M.C., T.F., assumes command of unit as from 18/1/18. Bearers of 2/1st H.F.Ambce. returned from A.D.S. to rejoin their unit.	
	19-1-18.		Bearers of 1/3rd H.F.Ambce. returned from A.D.S. to rejoin their unit.	
	20-1-18.		Relief of all personnel in forward area by Field Ambulances of 6th Division completed today. Second advance party under charge of Captain Mallace proceeded to Achiet-le-Grand.	
	21-1-18.		Unit moved from Beugny to Achiet-le Grand, and took over billets occupied by 1/3rd H.F.Ambulance. Hospital opened for treatment of Brigade sick.	
Achiet-le -Grand.	23-1-18.		Following notifications received. (a) Major G.W. Miller, D.S.O. has been appointed to command the 1/2nd Highland Field Ambulance. (Auty. Third Army No. A/A 10506 19/1/18.) (b) Major G.W. Miller. D.S.O. has been appointed Lieut. Colonel whilst commanding 1/2nd Highland Field Ambulance. (Auty. 51st H.D. No. 160/A. dated 22/1/18.	

Army Form C.2118.

WAR DIARY
of
INTELLIGENCE SUMMARY

(Erase heading not required.)

1/2nd Highland Field Ambulance, R.A.M.C., T.F.

Vol. 33. (2)

Place	Date	Hour	Summary of Events and Information	Remarks and references to Appendices
Achiet-le-Grand.	24-1-18		Captain Browne granted leave to Etaples 24th to 27th January. Captain Meighan reported for duty with D.D.M.S., IVth Corps in relief of Captain Milne, 1/3 H.F.A.	[initials]
	25-1-18.		A Dinner and Concert was held in the Y.M.C.A. hut, Achiet-le-Grand in celebration of "Burn's Night". (Copy of programme attached.)	[initials]
	27-1-18.		An Officer is detailed to visit and superintend the working of the Decauville Detraining Centre daily in relief of an Officer of the 6th Division.	[initials]
	28&29-1-18.		Throughout the nights 28/29 and 29/30th. the area was visited by enemy aircraft and several bombs dropped in the vicinity.	

31st. January, 1918.

George W Milne.
Lieutenant Colonel,
O.C., 1/2nd Highland Field Ambulance, R.A.M.C., T.F..

1/2nd Highland Field Ambulance, R.A.M.C., T.F.,

BURNS ANNIVERSARY..................25th. January, 1918.
   (held in hut kindly lent by Y.M.C.A.)

CHAIRMAN: Lieut. Col. G.W. MILLER, D.S.B..

Chairman's Remarks.

   Dinner................5-15p.m.
   Tea...................8-0 p.m.

CONCERT PROGRAMME.

Violin Selections.   Ptes. Reid, Rennie and Purves.

   Taffy's got his Jenny in Glamorgan.
   Waltz.
   Yamahula.

Chorus.........."The Star o' ROBBIE BURNS"
Solo............"Roamin' in the gloamin'"   Pte. Saunders.
Violin Solo..."Barcarolle"   Pte. Reid.
       (Songs of Hoffmann).
Solo............"Gae bring tae me
               a pint o' Wine"   Pte. Euman. (R.Scots).
Duet........."The ghost of the violin"   Ptes. Stewart and Foster.
Recitation..."Tam o' Shanter"   Pte. Platt. (R.Scots).
Solo........."Mountain Lovers"   Pte. Arnold.
Melody in F.   (Rubenstein)   Pte Rennie.
Humourous Song..............................Pte. McLeod.(8.Amb. Tr.).
Chorus...........Medley.
Bagpipe Selections........"Scotch Airs"   Pte. Euman. (R.Scots).
Solo........."Sunshine of your Smile"   Pte. Webster.
Violin Selections......"Gipsy Love"   " s.Reid, Rennie, & Purves.
Solo................"I love Jack"   Pte. Gray.
Dancing Exhibition......Highland Fling   Piper Dodds. (R.Scots).
                        Sword Dance
Solo..........."I'm for ords"   Pte. Foster.
Solo..........."When ola Bill Bailey"   Pte. Stewart.
Chorus...........Medley.
   "Auld Lang Syne"

GOD SAVE THE KING.

         Menu --------Dinner.
   Soup............Scotch Broth.
   Entree..........Steak Pie, Potatoes,
                   Brussells Sprouts and green peas.
   Sweet...........Tapioca Blanc Mange.
                   Custard.
   Dessert.........Fruit.
       Cigarettes.

Hurst Highland F.A.

COMMITTEE FOR THE
MEDICAL HISTORY OF THE WAR
Date —8 APR. 1918

WAR DIARY
INTELLIGENCE SUMMARY.

Army Form C. 2118.

Vol 3
Vol. N4 (1)

1/3 (Lothian) Brigade (Erase heading not required) Andre R.A.M.C.T.

Place	Date	Hour	Summary of Events and Information	Remarks and references to Appendices
Achiet-le-Grand.	1/2/18 -11/2/18		Working Hospital for treatment of Brigade Sick	gmm
	1/2/18		Lieut Shannon is detailed to report to 1/9 R Scots as temporary M.O. Weather Fine.	gmm
	2/2/18		No 61464 Corpe Babcon. C. sent to England for admission to Officers Cadet School. Weather fine.	gmm
	3/2/18		- do -	gmm
	4/2/18		33 O.R. detailed to report to O.C. No 3 C.C. Stn for Convalescent work. Weather Fine.	gmm
	5/2/18		do	gmm
	6/2/18		do	gmm
	7/2/18		do	gmm
	8/2/18		The unit Troupe "The Granite Chips" gave their first performance in Y.M.C.A. Hut, Achiet-le-Grand. Weather Dull & Stormy	gmm
	9/2/18		Working Party at No 3 C.C.Stn rejoined unit. Weather Dull & Stormy.	gmm
Bihucourt.	10/2/18		Advance Party consisting of tent subdivision proceeded to Rest Stn. Weather Dull	gmm

WAR DIARY
INTELLIGENCE SUMMARY.

1/3 F[?]y[?]d Ambce R.A.M.C.T

Army Form C. 2118.

Vol 24 (1)

Place	Date	Hour	Summary of Events and Information	Remarks and references to Appendices
Achiet le Grand	11/2/18		D.M.S., Third Army, made inspection of Camp. Weather mild.	appx.
	12/2/18		Unit moved to Behucourt and took over IV Corps Rest Stn from 17 Fd Ambce (532 patients taken over) weather dull.	appx.
Behucourt	13/2/18		Weather dull with rain.	appx.
	14/2/18		Sent sick [?] apps No 29 G.G. Stn (Keu 2 men) rejoined unit. Weather mild	appx.
	15/2/18		Lt Col A.G. Wallace to be a/feet 6th wheel Commanding 1/3 H.F.F.Amb from 8th to 18th Jany 1918 (Authority List No 170 of appointments, 70) Weather frosty	appx.
	16/2/18		do.	
	17/2/18		Enemy aircraft [?] dropped several bombs in vicinity weather fine.	appx.
	18/2/18		Information received that A.M.S. Mackay C. had been appointed Temporary Quartermaster as from 14.2.18 and asking him to report at Training Centre, Blackpool. A Medical School of Instruction was opened at IV Corps Rest Stn Behucourt (Copy of Syllabus attached).	appx.

Army Form C. 2118.

Vol 34 (11)

WAR DIARY
of
INTELLIGENCE SUMMARY.

1/2 Skigh (Erase heading not required) see R.A.M.C.T

Instructions regarding War Diaries and Intelligence Summaries are contained in F. S. Regs., Part II. and the Staff Manual respectively. Title pages will be prepared in manuscript.

Place	Date	Hour	Summary of Events and Information	Remarks and references to Appendices
Béhencourt	18/7/18		One officer & two other ranks detailed to attend IV Corps School of Instruction at Béhencourt week commencing 18/7/18. Reinforcement was made with inoculation of personnel at the rate of five per day. Weather fine.	9 mm
	19/7/18		do	9 mm
	20/7/18		Weather dull with rain	9 mm
	21/7/18		Weather fine	9 mm
	22/7/18		Three O.R. reported from No. 2 of IV Corps for one week's instruction in first aid. Weather fine	9 mm
	23/7/18		do	9 mm
	24/7/18		Weather dull	9 mm
	25/7/18		Weather stormy. Second Course of Lectures commenced (for officers only) (Copy of Syllabus attached)	9 mm
	26/7/18		Weather dull & stormy with rain.	9 mm
	27/7/18		Weather dull	9 mm
	28/7/18			9 mm

Army Form C. 2118.

WAR DIARY
or
INTELLIGENCE SUMMARY.
(Erase heading not required.)

Place	Date	Hour	Summary of Events and Information	Remarks and references to Appendices
			Note. The general health of the personnel of unit during the month of February was very good. The rations supplied were of excellent quality with a good proportion of bread & fresh meat. The billeting accommodation was also good. George W. M. Allen LIEUT. COL., R.A.M.C., T.F. O.C. 1/2nd HIGHLAND FIELD AMBULANCE	

II Corps Medical School. Syllabus of Lectures. 18/2/18 to 23/2/18.

	9 a.m. – 10 a.m.	10 a.m. – 11 a.m.	11 a.m. – 12.30 p.m.	2 p.m. – 3 p.m.	3 p.m. – 4 p.m.
Monday	Introductory lecture. Col. J. Hock. C.B. D.D.M.S. IV Corps	Orderly Room, Military Laws, Kings Regulations	Medical Organisation. Col. H. W. Grattan D.S.O. A.D.M.S. 6th Division	Wounds & their treatment. Capt Alexander RAMC No 3. C.C.S.	Water supplies. Capt. M. Leslie RAMC (T.F.) No. 14 San. Section
Tuesday	Organisation of Divisions Corps, Armies L. of C. etc. Col. N. M. Dunn D.S.O. A.D.M.S. 25th Division	Do.	Officers routine correspondence etc. Lieut Col. F. W. Miller D.S.O. O.C. 1/2nd (H) Field Amb.	Application of Splints Capt. Alexander RAMC No 3 C.C.S.	Sanitation of in Lieut J. W. Hollin RAMC (T.F.) O.C. No. 10 San. Section
Wednesday	Duties of R.M.O. on march & in camp. Lt. Col. W. Lynell D.S.O, M.C. C. de G. O.C. 76 Field Amb.	Do.	Organisation of a C.C.S. Lt Col. M. B. Ray D.S.O. O.C. No. 3. C.C.S.	"Shock" Capt. K. M. Walker RAMC at No. 20 C.C.S.	Sanitation of a unit at rest. Capt. M. Gribbin RAMC (T.F.) O.C. No 14 San. Section
Thursday	Duties of R.M.O. in the line. Capt. K. W. Jones D.S.O. M.O. 1st The Buffs	Do.	Organisation of a Field Ambulance. Col. D. Rorie D.S.O. A.D.M.S. 51st Division	"Gas" Capt. N. S. Oaten, Chemical Adviser IV Corps.	Demonstration of sick house at M.N. Deen 3.30 p.m.
Friday	Duties of Sanitary Officer in Field Ambulance. Col. D. Rorie D.S.O. A.D.M.S. 51st Division	Do.	Inoculation, Trench Feet. Inspection of Drafts. Capt. P. Mathew-Green RAMC	Clinical Demonstration at No 3. C.C.S.	Lecture by Col. H. M. W. Gray C.B. Consulting Surgeon Third Army
Saturday	Equipment, and how to replenish supplies. Hon. Lt. & Qmr S.R.L. Johnston 1/2nd (H) Field Amb.	Do.	Horsemanship. Col. G. J. McDavis D.S.O. A.D.V.S. IV Corps	Clinical Demonstration of cases at Rest Station. Capt A. C. Wallace 1/2nd (H) Field Amb.	Diagnosis of Scabies & allied skin affections. M.O. I/C Scabies Ward. Rest Station.

IV Corps Medical School. Syllabus of Lectures 25/2/18 to 2/3/18.

	2.30 p.m. – 3.30 p.m.	3.30 p.m. – 4.30 p.m.
Monday	Medical Organisation. Organisation of Divisions, Corps, Armies, L. of C. etc. Col. H.N. Dunn, D.S.O., A.D.M.S. 35th Division.	Equipment & how to replenish supplies. Claims against Public. Lt. & Qmr. R.S. Johnston RAMC.(T) 1/3rd (H) Fd Amb.
Tuesday	Duties of R.M.O. in Camp & on the march. Lt Col. H. Lynch, D.S.O., C. de G., O.C. 76th Field Amb.	Duties of R.M.O. in the Line. Capt. L.H. Jones, D.S.O. R.A.M.C. M.O. 1/C 10th Lil Suffs.
Wednesday	Duties of Senior Officers in Field Ambulances. Col. D. Cone, D.S.O., A.D.M.S. 51st (H) Division.	Inoculation, Trench Foot, Inspection of Drafts, Prevention of wastage. Capt. D. Withers - Green RAMC.
Thursday	Organisation of Field Ambulances & their disposition in offensive & defensive operations. Col. D. Cone, D.S.O. A.D.M.S. 51st (H) Division.	Wounded & their treatment. "Shock" Capt. Alexander R.A.M.C. No 3 C.C.S.
Friday	Sanitation of the Line, and of a unit at rest.	Elementary Military Law. Lt. & Qmr. R.S. Johnston R.A.M.C.(T) 1/3rd (H) Field Ambulance.
Saturday	"Gas" Capt. H.L. Oaten, Chemical Adviser IV Corps	Application of Splints & Demonstration at No 3 C.C.S. Capt. Alexander R.A.M.C. No 3 C.C.S.

March 1918

1/2 Argyll & S.A.

40/2649

COMMITTEE FOR THE
OFFICIAL HISTORY OF THE WAR
Date 12 MAY 1918

Army Form C. 2118.

Vol 35 (1)

WAR DIARY
of
INTELLIGENCE SUMMARY.

1/2 Highland Field Ambulance R.A.M.C.T.

No 35

Place	Date	Hour	Summary of Events and Information	Remarks and references to Appendices
Frevin	1/3/18	23/2/18	Working W Capt. Rest Station at Bihucourt. Dryhead weather, working well.	9mm.
	1/3/18		Capt Melvin returned from leave.	9mm.
	2/3/18		Party of 40 O.R. proceeded to report for duty to O.C. 2/1 H.F. Amb.	9mm.
			Major MacIntosh reported for duty from Rest Camp Étretat.	9mm.
			Heavy gale of wind. Shorthand renew.	
	3/3/18		D.O.M.S. delivered lecture at School of Instruction, Rest Station.	
	4/3/18		Capt Melvin detailed as temp'y M.O. of 1st Seat Highrs.	9mm.
	5/3/18		Capt Browne detailed as temp'y M.O. of 1/7 R.I. Highrs.	9mm.
	6/3/18		Three horsed Ambces with drivers sent to report for dutywith 1/3 H.F.Amb. Four Cars sent to report for duty with 2/1 H.F.Amb. Obtained clean supply of straw for filling of paillasses to replace stretchers in wards	9mm.
	7/3/18		Capt. Mallace detailed as temp'y M.O. at V.A.C.	9mm.
			Capt Browne returned to unit from 1/7 R.I. Highrs.	9mm.
	9/3/18		Officers attended lecture at Mob. Vet Section, Bapaume	9mm.
	10/3/18		Reached R.A.S.M.S. re arrangement for lorries to go up line.	9mm.
			27 O.R. sent to report for duty with 2/1 H.F.Amb	9mm.
	11/3/18		Capt Neighan proceeded on leave. Authority granted to Capt Mallace to wear rank of Major, while present appointment.	9mm.
	12/3/18		D.D.M.S. visited Rest Sta. re expected advance. Received advice 1928 blankets per day for division.	9mm.
	13/3/18		Lt Johnstone returned from leave. Continuous fine weather.	9mm.

Army Form C. 2118.

WAR DIARY
of
INTELLIGENCE SUMMARY.
(Erase heading not required.)

1/3 Highland Field Ambce R.A.M.C.

Vol. N5 (11)

Instructions regarding War Diaries and Intelligence Summaries are contained in F. S. Regs., Part II. and the Staff Manual respectively. Title pages will be prepared in manuscript.

Place	Date	Hour	Summary of Events and Information	Remarks and references to Appendices
Field	18/3/18		Half acre of spare land at Rest Station ploughed in addition to previous 5mm area planted. IV Corps Agricultural Officer called re delivery of seeds for same. 1 piece of delouser turned out. Revues dans. W.P. Lieut. Philip reported for duty with unit.	5mm
	19/3/18		D.M.S. Third Army called in forenoon & inspected delouser. Gen. Sir W. Herringham and D.D.M.S. IV Corps called in afternoon and took away every shirt which had been treated in disinfector for experimental purposes.	5mm
	20/3/18		Capt Melvin rejoined from 1/4 Sea. Hghrs.	5mm
	21/3/18		Heavy artillery bombardment commenced about midnight with enemy aeroplane bombing in neighbourhood. Surface bombardment about 3.30am. all along front. Achiet le Grand shelled from 4.30am to 8.30am. Heavy casualties in C.C.Sms. there. Capt Browne Lieut. Chieph reported to R.O.M.S. for duty at Bergues and Ferbuguieres. Capt Melvin reported for duty to 1/3 H.F.A.M.B 20 O.R. reported for duty to 2/1 H.F.A.M.B. Lt. Col. Robertson 2/1 H.F.Ambce killed in action at Ferbuguieres	5mm
	22/3/18		Main dressing returned from Bergues to Loch Camp. Achiet le Grand shelled in morning. Unit moved from Loch Camp to Frevillers. Arrived on front quieter in afternoon.	5mm

Army Form C. 2118.

WAR DIARY
of
INTELLIGENCE SUMMARY.
(Erase heading not required.)

Vol 35 (III)
1/8 Field Ambulance R.A.M.C. T.

Instructions regarding War Diaries and Intelligence Summaries are contained in F.S. Regs., Part II. and the Staff Manual respectively. Title pages will be prepared in manuscript.

Place	Date	Hour	Summary of Events and Information	Remarks and references to Appendices
Field	23/3/18		Achiet a Grand shelled in morning. Capt. Browne reported from front area as not being required and sent to report to A.D.M.S.	(I.V.V)
		9am	A.D.M.S. called during forenoon shook Major Mashtabah for duty at Main Dressing Station, Grevillers. Rest Station shelled and 3 patients killed & 1 wounded. At same time order was received from A.D.M.S. to retire to Puisieux. All preparations had been made to evacuate, in forenoon and en-route (9IVVI). Moved out half hour after getting order, taking all remaining patients (300 in number) the route taken being cross country via Achiet to Petit. Transport went by road that gave great difficulty owing to bad condition of road. I rode on in advance to secure billets where else for camp. Returning afterwards to meet transport. Pitched tents for hospital and dressed all surgical cases. Received word from A.D.M.S. to reconnoitre Beaucourt for site for Main Dressing Station.	
	24/3/18		Proceeded to Beaucourt in car and after choosing a site reported to A.D.M.S. at Grevillers, then returned to Puisieux. Q.M. returned to Rest Stn, Behucourt to arrange for salvage of stores left behind.	(I.V.V.I)
		9pm	The 3 patients killed at Rest Stn. were buried at Puisieux. Field Ambce. & camp at Puisieux and marched to Beaucourt.	

A 8534. Wt. W.4973 M687 750,000. 8/16 D, D, & L, Ltd. Forms/C.2118/13.

Army Form C. 2118.

WAR DIARY
of
INTELLIGENCE SUMMARY.
(Erase heading not required.)

Vol XV (iv)

13th Field Ambulance R.A.M.C. T.

Instructions regarding War Diaries and Intelligence Summaries are contained in F.S. Regs., Part II. and the Staff Manual respectively. Title pages will be prepared in manuscript.

Place	Date	Hour	Summary of Events and Information	Remarks and references to Appendices
Field	24/3/18		Reorganised with 1/3 & 1/1 Fd Ambce at Beaucourt. Picketted all available canvas. Capt Melvin & Phillips sent to report to Bde HQrs & 1/6 Sea Highrs respectively. Could not find them returned to camp. Handed our steering gear to 1/3 Fd Ambce immediately completed. About 10 p.m. orders arrived to move at once to Authieulles. Struck camp and moved off before midnight. 300 patients still marching with unit. Arrived Authieulles about 1 a.m. Night clear & frosty with bright moonlight. All ranks slept in open.	(MM)
	25/3/18		Went by car after breakfast to report to ADMS. at Beauquesne, and was instructed to send L. Phillips to report to Bde HQrs at Sus. Arranged to evacuate patients by empty returning supply train. Capts Bourne & Melvin marched 212 patients to Courcamps & handed them over to R.T.O. there. The remainder being fit for duty were retained. In afternoon got tickets for officers R.T. on leave. A steady stream of troops kept retiring past camp all day. About 5.30 pm. This had ceased all transport having left area. At that time the infantry were along Beaumont Hamel ridge. The enemy was on other side of Ancre. Some shells burst in close proximity to field where unit was lying. No orders having been received the Field Ambulance Commanders decided to march and marched via Mailly Maillet	(MM) (MM) (MM)

A 5834 Wt. W.4973 M687 750,000 8/16 D.D. & L., Ltd. Forms/C.2118/13.

Army Form C. 2118.

WAR DIARY
or
INTELLIGENCE SUMMARY
(Erase heading not required.)

Vol 35 (V)

Place	Date	Hour	Summary of Events and Information	Remarks and references to Appendices
Field	23/3/18		Beaurevoir. Orders received on march to proceed to Bertrancourt. The three units parted there. 17/3 H.F.A.M.B. evacuated large number of wounded. Commenced to pitch tents & prepare for personnel when orders arrived to move at once to Henu. The march was very difficult owing to roads being bad & up placed. Leaving Arbeoy had to turn three horses officially marched via Bus & Acheux. Arrived at Henu 11.30 p.m. from billets last night. Everything promised a quiet day. Suddenly at 11 a.m. transport began to pour through village and however galloped over the field. Officers were reported that enemy cavalry was at Sauxtre. Fell in men at once and decided to march off. Great difficulty experienced on road with huge banking of traffic recovered wagons. Marched via PAS to Mondicourt where orders were received from A.D.M.S to proceed to SAULTY.	J.M.M
	26/3/18		Transport consistently broken up on road by vehicles breaking in. Our portion was diverted by side track to avoid PAS village. While going through a wood Arbia wagon locked in a tree three had to be cawer down to elevate wagon. Lorry cart was upset by tree & has recovered & had to be abandoned. This portion of transport rejoined Column & Co.	J.M.M

WAR DIARY
of
INTELLIGENCE SUMMARY

(Erase heading not required.)

Army Form C. 2118.

Vol 25 (VI)

72 Field Amb. A.I.F. C.T

Place	Date	Hour	Summary of Events and Information	Remarks and references to Appendices
Field	26/3/18		Halted at Sandy Hill whole Column closed up and then moved on and parked in first available field on South side of Sombrin village. A.D.M.S. called in evening. Ambce Car returned to Herve to collect stores left there. Good billets for night in Sombrin village. Lt Philip rejoined unit.	G.M.W.
	27/3/18		Marched from Sombrin at 10am via Sus St Leger, Sivigny, and Bouquemaison to Newiette. Halted at Sivigny to feed riverhorses. Good billets secured for night at La Caverie Farm. A.D.M.S. called in evening.	G.M.W.
	28/3/18		Roll call made in morning & 3 N.C.Os + 36 men found to be missing. These men were supposed to be captured by enemy at Beauvois Sus 2 Major Ambce Cars also took at A.D.M.S. Q.M.S. went to Beauval for Med Stores returned unsuccessful equipment to rail-head.	G.M.W.
	29/3/18		Called at A.D.M.S for orders. Personnel had very enjoyable concert in evening. Orders arrived to march following day. Loaded wagon in morning. Capt Browne proceeded with Ambce Cars of 3 circles to new area at 9am	G.M.W.

A5334 Wt. W4973 M687 750,000 8/16 D. D. & L. Ltd. Forms/C.2118/13.

Army Form C. 2118.

WAR DIARY
of
INTELLIGENCE SUMMARY.
79 Highland Field Amb. R.A.M.C.T. Vol X5 (VII)
(Erase heading not required.)

Place	Date	Hour	Summary of Events and Information	Remarks and references to Appendices
Field	29/3/18		Lieuts Johnstone & Thicap marched with transport at 9am. Personnel marched at 1pm via Bouquemaison & Frevent. Marched past Icrig in Bouquemaison & recap. Fell out Frequent name of unit and destination. During unit to train at Frevent tea was made supplied to personnel. Entrained about 7pm.	9pm.
	30/3/18		Arrived Saizncong 1am. Detrained marched to Sorney. Billeted in Chateau formerly used as I Corps School of Instruction. A.D.M.S along with W.A.D.M.S I Corps called in afternoon. Proceeded with them to Arregin to inspect Ambee site there. Ordered by A.D.M.S to move in following day. Capt. Meighen received wire from leave.	9pm.
	31/3/18		Marched at 9am via Bethune to Arregin and occupied Field Ambee site there. Unloaded wagons repacked wards ready for reception of sick of Division.	9pm.

A5834 Wt. W4973/M687 750,000 8/16 D.D.&L.Ltd. Forms/C.2118/13.

Army Form C. 2118.

WAR DIARY
of
INTELLIGENCE SUMMARY.
(Erase heading not required.)

1/2 Highland Field Ambulance R.A.M.C. T

Vol 35 (VIII)

Place	Date	Hour	Summary of Events and Information	Remarks and references to Appendices
			Note:— As a result of the rapid continuous marching of the last week of the month a considerable amount of equipment is missing. The men are tired and clothing rather ragged and dirty. The vehicles (horse & M.T.) are also shewing signs of wear and rough usage. The horses are in very good order as also is the harness. George W Miller LIEUT. COL., R.A.M.C., T.F. O.C. 1/2nd HIGHLAND FIELD AMBULANCE	8mm

1 APR 1918
1/2nd HIGHLAND FIELD AMBULANCE
R.A.M.C. (T.) B.E.F.

160/2900.

1/2nd Highland Field Ambulance.

COMMITTEE FOR THE
MEDICAL HISTORY OF THE WAR
Date −6 JUN.1918

WAR DIARY

INTELLIGENCE SUMMARY

Army Form C. 2118.

1/2 Field 2nd Cav[alry]
R.A.M.C.T.
Vol. 36 (1)

Place	Date	Hour	Summary of Events and Information	Remarks and references to Appendices
Auxi-gun	1/4/18		Working Hospital for treatment of sick of Division. Made inspection of A.S.C. Horse Transport.	9mm
	2/4/18		Commenced clearing training of waggons. By order of A.D.M.S. I proceeded to NOEUX les MINES and VERQUIGNEUX and reconnoitred possible collecting posts for defence scheme. Left one N.C.O. and 6 men in charge of waggons. Reported return to A.D.M.S. on return.	9mm
	3/4/18		G.O.C. Division inspected Hospital today. Two new Talbot Ambulance Cars arrived from Workshops. Three officers proceeded to MOEUX les MINES to go over ground for possible Advanced Dressing Station.	9mm
	4/4/18		Orders were received at 2 a.m. to move to MARLES les MINES. Capt. Browne proceeded in advance with billeting party. Unit moved off at 10.30 am via LABEUVRIERE and LAPUGNOY and arrived MARLES les MINES at 1.30 p.m. Orderly Officer stayed behind to arrange for disposal of Brigade sick and Venereal cases, &c.	9mm

Army Form C. 2118.

WAR DIARY
INTELLIGENCE SUMMARY.
(Erase heading not required.)

VOL 36 (m)
R.A.M.C.T

Instructions regarding War Diaries and Intelligence Summaries are contained in F. S. Regs., Part II. and the Staff Manual respectively. Title pages will be prepared in manuscript.

Place	Date	Hour	Summary of Events and Information	Remarks and references to Appendices
Field	4/4/18		Very scattered billets. No suitable place for Hospital. Brigadier General, 152 Inf. Brigade called in evening. Arrangement of billets made in morning.	4mm
	5/4/18	1.30 pm	Received warning order from Brigade to move. Billeting party to report to Brigade HQrs at once.	4mm
		2.40 pm	Operation order received to be clear of billets at 2.30 pm. Marched out at 3 pm en route for HAM en ARTOIS. Part of Infantry followed behind unit.	
			On arrival at HAM in ARTOIS no billets were available so unit moved on to CORNET BOURDOIS. Capt Browne goes to Brigade HQ Qrs to arrange about new billets.	4mm
	6/4/18		R.A.M.C. and W.A.A.M.C. arrived at 12.30 pm.	4mm
	7/4/18	1 pm	Marched to CANTRAINNE. New ford car arrives from workshop. Billets very good. Wagons parked on road for night. Parked wagons in a field. Arranged dressing room and Medical Inspection Room.	4mm

Army Form C. 2118.

Vol 36 (111)

WAR DIARY
of
INTELLIGENCE SUMMARY.
(Erase heading not required.)

1/1 West Lancs F.A. R.A.M.C.T.

Instructions regarding War Diaries and Intelligence Summaries are contained in F. S. Regs., Part II. and the Staff Manual respectively. Title pages will be prepared in manuscript.

Place	Date	Hour	Summary of Events and Information	Remarks and references to Appendices
Fieus	7/4/18		New Talbot Ambulance Car arrived from workshop. Major Mallam reported sick from 51 D.R.S.	AMM
	8/4/18		A social evening was held in Sergt. Mess. Capt. Thompson E.G. and Capt. Moore, B.S., R.A.M.C., reported for duty. Wagon loads were readjusted. Ordnance stores to replace those lost in retreat commenced to arrive.	AMM
	9/4/18		A party of 50 O.R. sent to report for duty to O.C. 1/3 W.L. Amb. Received order from A.D.M.S. to report with two Medical Officers for duty at A.D.M.S. Personnel and equipment to be supplied by 1/3 W.L. Amb. Proceeded with Capt. McEwen & Capt. Meghan to ROBECQ and reported to A.D.M.S., thereafter going with A.D.M.S. via COLONNE towards ZELOBES. Met O.C. 1/6 Sea. Highrs. at R.25.c.5.9. (Sheet 36 a) who informed us we could not go further forward.	AMM

1577 Wt.W10791/1773 500,000 1/15 D. D. & L. A.D.S.S./Forms/C. 2118.

Army Form C. 2118.

VOL N6 (IV)

WAR DIARY
or
INTELLIGENCE SUMMARY
(Erase heading not required)

R.A.M.C.T

Place	Date	Hour	Summary of Events and Information	Remarks and references to Appendices
Izeed	9/4/18		Got in touch with 152 Inf Bde Hd Qrs and found ADMS at Farm House, R.25.c.3.3.	
			Capt Meighen reported to Brigade as Liaison Officer.	
			Heavily shelled all afternoon.	
			Rapid evacuating all wounded as all available cars by three to cars returned until 3pm when Divisional Cars and 6 M.A.C. Cars reported. This delay was due to the fact that the Divisional Cars were being sent all the way to the C.C. Stn. with patients.	S.M.M
			During this period there was also a shortage of stretchers and blankets which I was expecting up with returning cars.	
	5:30 p.m.		Major Wallace reported with extra bearers, medical stores, stretchers and blankets, so a sufficiency of these was now on the spot.	
			I left the A.D.S.Stn. and reported to A.D.M.S. at To B.S.Q.	S.M.M
			Report by Major Wallace attached to all the appendices	

WAR DIARY

INTELLIGENCE SUMMARY

Army Form C. 2118.

Vol. JG (V)

R.A.M.C.T.

Place	Date	Hour	Summary of Events and Information	Remarks and references to Appendices
Iseel	10/4/18		Went to Busnes to see O.C. 1/3 H.J.Ambce. re Cars. Reported again to A.D.M.S. Thereafter returning to Busnes and to A.D.M.S. to find out where Main Dressing Stn was to open. Proceeded to both A.D.Stns. Saw Major Tunker with 1/3 H.J.Amb. A.D.Stn. at Q.23.c.3.8. Called at 152 Bde. Hd. Qrs. at Q.23.d.0.1. and then at 1/2 H.J.Amb. A.D.Stn. which had moved that morning to R.25.b.0.9. Apart from certain unavoidable delays in removing of cars evacuation had been proceeding smoothly and both A.D.Stns were practically clear. Then reported to A.D.M.S. and returned to Hd Qrs of 1/3 H.J.Amb. in afternoon. By this time Main Dressing Stn. had been established at P.26.b.5.2.	S.N.M.
	11/4/18		A party of 12 O.R. proceeded for duty to A.D.Stn. from end. Reported to A.D.M.S. at 8.30 am. Informed that Capt Meenie party from A.D.Stn at R.25.b.0.9. had retired to cause bank at P.30.c.6.1.	S.N.M.

Army Form C. 2118.

VOL 26 (VI)

WAR DIARY
INTELLIGENCE SUMMARY.
(Erase heading not required.)

R.A.M.C.T.

Instructions regarding War Diaries and Intelligence Summaries are contained in F. S. Regs., Part II. and the Staff Manual respectively. Title pages will be prepared in manuscript.

Place	Date	Hour	Summary of Events and Information	Remarks and references to Appendices
Field	11/4/18		Major Wallace referred to CORNET MALO. Cars wanted urgently to switched on 6 M.A.C. cars from Main dressing Stn. All posts reported clear at 2.30 p.m. M.A.C. cars taken off. Ordered Capt. Browne, Capt. Thompson, Lieut. Cheirip to report to me at Canal Bank. Received Capt. Mecain. Hd Qrs of unit moved to CORNET BOURDOIS. Main dressing Stn moved to BUSNES Chateau. Took two Ford cars up COLONNE road in evening to collect some wounded reported to be there and returned to Hd Qrs of 1/3 H.J. Ambces at BUSNES Chateau.	g.m.m.
	12/4/18	9am	Major Wallace reported to me at BUSNES Chateau along with Major Herbert, Capt. Browne, Capt. Moore and Capt. Thompson. They report rapid advance of enemy; 152 Brigade Hd Qrs, with Capt. Meighan cut off meaning	g.m.m.

1577 Wt. W10791/1773 500,000 1/15 D. D. & L. A.D.S.S./Forms/C. 2118.

Army Form C. 2118.

Vol 36 (VII)

WAR DIARY
INTELLIGENCE SUMMARY.
(Erase heading not required.)

~~Mobile Section~~ R.A.M.C.T.

Instructions regarding War Diaries and Intelligence Summaries are contained in F. S. Regs., Part II. and the Staff Manual respectively. Title pages will be prepared in manuscript.

Place	Date	Hour	Summary of Events and Information	Remarks and references to Appendices
Field	10/4/18		The Telephone. A. Driver of Ford Ambce cars was captured with McCoy's ford. Thigho but they subsequently escaped. Ford Car was lost.	
		10 am	Capt. Thompson and Lieut. Phillips are sent with cars to ROBECQ to collect any wounded there. They report none. They then proceeded to the bridge on the BUSNES - ST. VENANT road and got into touch with 153 Brigade Hrs Qrs at L'EPINETTE. P. 20. C. 1. 9.	S.M.M.
			Main dressing Stn moved to HAM en ARTOIS.	
			R.A.P.Stn. established at BUSNES Chateau.	
		11:30 am	Lieut Phillips and bearers remain at Brigade H.Q. Qrs. at L'EPINETTE.	
			Saw D.A.D.M.S XI Corps at New Hd.Qrs in afternoon and pointed out where dressing stn and stretcher stns was. All officers except myself, Capt. Browne + Capt. Moore returned to their units. Hd. Qrs. of unit moved to FONTES.	S.M.M.

Army Form C. 2118.

Vol 36 (VIII)

WAR DIARY
of
INTELLIGENCE SUMMARY.
(Erase heading not required.)

[Field Ambulance] R.A.M.C.

Instructions regarding War Diaries and Intelligence Summaries are contained in F. S. Regs., Part II. and the Staff Manual respectively. Title pages will be prepared in manuscript.

Place	Date	Hour	Summary of Events and Information	Remarks and references to Appendices
Field	12/4/18		Visited Main Dressing Stn. at HAM en ARTOIS in afternoon and returned to BUSNES. A draft of 150 O.R. arrived at BUSNES Chateau for distribution to three Field Ambulances. Lorries arrived with stretchers and blankets for II Corps. Arranged loading party for same. Capt. Moore is sent at Liason Officer with Fleming's force to Brigade Hd Qrs at P.22.c.3.3. with one ambulance car and motor cycle. Personnel of 12th Field Ambulance arrived at BUSNES Chateau and billeted for the night. Capt Moore & Lieut. Philp reported to me in morning. All quiet on front. G.O.C. 51 Division inspected R.D.Stn. Quiet day. O.C. 1/3 Highd. Fd Amble called in afternoon.	gmm
	13/4/18			

1577 Wt. W10791/1773 500,000 1/15 D. D. & L. A.D.S.S./Forms/C. 2118.

WAR DIARY
INTELLIGENCE SUMMARY.
(Erase heading not required.)

Army Form C. 2118.

Vol 36 (IX)

R.A.M.C.

Place	Date	Hour	Summary of Events and Information	Remarks and references to Appendices
Field	13/4/18		No 12 Lt Amb.'s marched out in evening and reinforcements for 2/1 N.Z.F.Amb and 1/3 N.Z.F.Amb were sent to join units. Capt. Irchig A.A.M.C (att 2/1 N.Z.F.Amb) reported to me for duty and was sent as R.M.O. to Battalion of Fleming's Force.	G.M.M.
	14/4/18	2 am	Two Ambulance Cars detached vis ROBECQ. Sent for First Aid lorry which arrived at 6.15 am and got cars out.	
		8 am	Capt. Browne visited R.A.P.s C.R.E. (O.C. Fleming's Force) does not want Divisional Officer. Sent A.D.M.S. orders or them being kept. D.D.M.S. XI Corps, visited Ad.Stn. Told him I had asked a large number of stretchers and blankets, and he arranged to send a lorry for them. Went to Mairi Dressing Stn. in afternoon for medical comforts, surgical instruments, rations, &c., and returned to BUSNES. Very quiet day. Heavy bombardment by our Artillery in evening.	G.M.M.

Army Form C. 2118.

WAR DIARY
INTELLIGENCE SUMMARY.
(Erase heading not required.)

[illegible] R.A.M.C.

Vol 36 (X)

Instructions regarding War Diaries and Intelligence Summaries are contained in F. S. Regs., Part II. and the Staff Manual respectively. Title pages will be prepared in manuscript.

Place	Date	Hour	Summary of Events and Information	Remarks and references to Appendices
Field	15/4/18		Called on A.D.M.S. in morning. Visited Aid Posts in ROBECQ and Capt. Thompson with me in relief of Capt. Moore as Liaison Officer to 154 Bde which relieved Kennedy's Force. Major MacIntosh and Capt. Meeun relieved Capt. Browne and myself who along with Capt. Moore, Lieut. Phillips returned to H.Q. Qrs. of unit at FONTES. All surplus bearers and cars of 1/3 H.F.A. and 1/3 H.F.A. returned from forward area to their units.	[illeg]
	16/4/18		Visited BUSNES Chateau in afternoon with Quartermaster. Evening and parties of wagons being provided with Received orders to return motor lorry which had been used at BUSNES for carrying wounded cases.	[illeg]
	17/4/18		Orders were received that a holding party was to be left at BUSNES Chateau & the unit moved out without being relieved.	[illeg]

Army Form C. 2118.

WAR DIARY
or
INTELLIGENCE SUMMARY.
(Erase heading not required.)

Vol 2 (XI)

Instructions regarding War Diaries and Intelligence Summaries are contained in F. S. Regs., Part II. and the Staff Manual respectively. Title pages will be prepared in manuscript.

Place	Date	Hour	Summary of Events and Information	Remarks and references to Appendices
Field	17/4/18		O.O.M.S. XI Corps, visited BUSNES Chateau this morning. Wished a topography of returned to be prepared for feeding of patients.	
	18/4/18		Submitted recommendations for training and awards.	9 MM
	19/4/18		Visited BUSNES Chateau in afternoon. D.D.M.S. XI Corps had called there at 7.30 am.	9 MM
	20/4/18		Went to St Omer and arranged about tracking the truckers, money.	9 MM
			Lieut Phelp received Capt. Thompson as Brigade H.Q Ors.	9 MM
	21/4/18		Visited Main Dressing Station at HAM and ROUSK, BUSNES Chateau. Arranged to receive personnel of 10 Ir Divs at ROUSK by men of this unit.	9 MM
			Got Registration of all personnel examined by divisional Gas officers.	
			11 C.C.S. proceeded to ROUSK in receipt of remaining Vice.	
	22/4/18		Accompanied A.D.M.S. to BUSNES Chateau.	9 MM
			20 C.C.S. proceeded in receipt to ROUSK	
	23/4/18		Visited BUSNES Chateau in morning, found all correct.	9 MM

(A7092) Wt. W12850/M1293. 750,000. 1/17. D. D. & L., Ltd. Forms/C.2118-14.

WAR DIARY
INTELLIGENCE SUMMARY

Army Form C. 2118.

Vol 36 (XII)

(Erase heading not required.)

Instructions regarding War Diaries and Intelligence Summaries are contained in F.S. Regs, Part II. and the Staff Manual respectively. Title pages will be prepared in manuscript.

Place	Date	Hour	Summary of Events and Information	Remarks and references to Appendices
Field	24/4/18		Major Wallace & Capt. Moore proceeded to BUSNES Chateau to relieve Major MacIntosh & Capt. Melvin. Major Philip returned to unit. No gas being sent over to Major Wallace to return to unit for training. Morning transport expected in evening. Very good turn out.	9/1/11
	25/4/18		Major Wallace & 450 Q returned to unit. Capt. Moore and 20 O.R. remaining at 100 Stn as holding party. In accordance with instructions from No. 9 M.S. XI Corps, 9 wheeled stretcher carriers were handed over to 6/10 Division.	9/1/11
	26/4/18		Visited BUSNES Chateau in morning	9/1/11
	27/4/18		Major Wallace visited BUSNES Chateau. Capt. Judge RC Chaplain attached to unit for duty.	9/1/11
	28/4/18		Visited BUSNES Chateau in morning and met Lt Col M.S. Cuming. Discussed you know what information & carted. Letter of reference by Capt. Melvin (Suspect) Arrival Shock (Prevention & Treatment)	9/1/11
	29/4/18		Received warning wait for news of Division from XI to XVII Corps. Called on 100 M.S. regarding holding party at BUSNES Chateau. Proceeded to BUSNES to warn Capt. Moore re movement to O/A Gr.	11 M

Army Form C. 2118.

Vol. 36 (XIII)

WAR DIARY
or
INTELLIGENCE SUMMARY.
(Erase heading not required.)

1/2nd Highland Field Ambulance R.A.M.C.T.

Instructions regarding War Diaries and Intelligence Summaries are contained in F. S. Regs., Part II. and the Staff Manual respectively. Title pages will be prepared in manuscript.

Place	Date	Hour	Summary of Events and Information	Remarks and references to Appendices
Field	29/4/18		Orders regarding move cancelled. Capt. Thompson received Capt Moore at Cat Shell Business. All personnel at rest, pers through gas hut (Suspect-Ipecacan.)	5 MM
			Lecture to personnel by Major Wallace (Subject - Inchages).	5 MM
	30/4/18		Lecture to personnel by Lieut Philips (Subject - Haemorrhage).	5 MM

George W. Mills
LIEUT. COL. R.A.M.C., T.F.
O.C. 1/2nd HIGHLAND FIELD AMBULANCE

1/2nd HIGHLAND FIELD AMBULANCE
1 MAY 1918
R.A.M.C. (T) B.E.F.

Army Form C. 2118.

WAR DIARY
of
INTELLIGENCE SUMMARY.
(Erase heading not required.)

1/2nd Highland Field Amb. R.A.M.C.T.

VOL 36 (X/V)

Instructions regarding War Diaries and Intelligence Summaries are contained in F. S. Regs., Part II. and the Staff Manual respectively. Title pages will be prepared in manuscript.

Place	Date	Hour	Summary of Events and Information	Remarks and references to Appendices
			Note The chief feature about recent operations as regards evacuation of wounded was the great success with which it was carried out in spite of the promises being greatly reduced in numbers. This reflects much credit on the officers in charge of AD.M.S. and the convoys working with them. The motor ambulances also did very good work which was rendered possible by the excellent state of the roads right up to the front line. One bad stretch in particular, by M20.5.9.48 Pt. Skyhey'd, Van hee's car continuously for several hours between the R.A.P. & Ford line and was the means of evacuating to Cpy. Rail of patients who would otherwise have had to be abandoned to the enemy. Evacuation of possible wounded during such month was never well advanced. During period of rest the personnel have undergone courses of physical drill with route march. They have been visited & very on various subjects by medical officers. With the exception of a few cases of P.U.O. the health of the unit has been excellent. Lieut W.M.W... Lieut Col., R.A.M.C. T.F. O.C. 1/2nd Highland Field Amb...	

1 MAY 1918

140/5983

1/2nd Highland F.A.

Retained

WAR DIARY or INTELLIGENCE SUMMARY

Army Form C. 2118.

Vol 37 (1)

...RAMC...

Vol 37

Place	Date	Hour	Summary of Events and Information	Remarks and references to Appendices
FONTES	1/5/18		Visited A.D.M.S. at BUSNES Chateau. Warning order received from Brigade for move of division	4pmn
	2/5/18		Reported to A.D.M.S. in forenoon. An inspection of kit was made in afternoon. A.S.C. officers called to obtain information regarding supply of Sodium Bisulph. necessary against Aube gas.	4pmn
	3/5/18		Visited A.D.V.S. at BUSNES, and called at Manoeuvres on way back. Col. J.B. M.C. reported with me at A.D.M.S. office in evening to arrange details of move.	4pmn
	4/5/18		Orders received from 152 Inf. Bde for transport to move on 4/5. Transport moved off at 9am under charge of Lt Johnstone en route for Brevet Toyecc. Called at 152 Bde HqQrs in evening concerning train entraining orders received. Stretcher carriers returned from 61 Division and one to Division by car.	4pmn
	5/5/18		Capt Browne & party proceeded by car to recce area to prepare billets. Unit marched off at 7.30am. Disembarking point at LAMBRES. at 8.35am. Entrained at AIRE. Train left AIRE at 10.30am. Brigade Capt Moore was detailed as entraining medical officer for Brigade	4pmn

Army Form C. 2118.

WAR DIARY
or
INTELLIGENCE SUMMARY.
(Erase heading not required.)

Vol 27 (11)

[unit heading] R.A.M.C.T.

Instructions regarding War Diaries and Intelligence Summaries are contained in F. S. Regs., Part II. and the Staff Manual respectively. Title pages will be prepared in manuscript.

Place	Date	Hour	Summary of Events and Information	Remarks and references to Appendices
Arca	5/5/18		Major Amies C.M.G. moved by road to new area under charge of Capt Thompson. Train arrived at A.C.G. at 5 p.m. Unit detrained and marched to billets in PREVENT CAPELLE. Following decorations are awarded by Corps Commander for gallantry. Bar to Military Medal No. 303626 Pte Allan G. 303011 Sgt Milne D.J. 543008 a/Sgt Garrow A.E. Military Medal 30.30.31 Pte Redden J. 30.32.76 Tracer J.S. 30.11.69 " Lamb. Geo.R.	gMM. gave iv award 1 May 1918
	6/5/18		Went in car to Mont St Eloy, then to Anzin Management to collect unit mails and rect from Battalion of 152 Inf Bde. A.D.M.S. called in afternoon. I proceeded on the line to 57 C.C. Stn AUBIGNY to connect the O.C. there regarding site for Divisional Rest Station.	gMM.
	7/5/18		Received orders to collect 10 marquees from trench at present 4 and 8 from Hank Avenues. Major MacIntosh and party went to Aubigny to fetch hospital. Transport sent for marquees.	gMM.

Army Form C. 2118.

WAR DIARY
or
INTELLIGENCE SUMMARY.
(Erase heading not required.)

Vol 37 (III)
1/2 [unclear] R.A.M.C.T

Place	Date	Hour	Summary of Events and Information	Remarks and references to Appendices
Ficed	7/5/18		I accompanied Major Maodonach to Aubigny to decide on site for Hospital. Then proceeded to A.D.M.S. office at Manueul.	g.M.M.
	8/5/18		A.D.M.S. called at midday. In afternoon took car to Manueul. Picked up A.D.M.S. and went to Corps H.Q. Ord. to see A.D.M.S. who was out. Proceeded to Aubigny and met him in 1/2 C.C. Stn. Went with A.D.M.S. to 57 C.C. Stn. to discuss dep[ar]ture for D.R. Stn. Got authority from A.D.M.S. to draw stretcher bearers &c. from Army at Hauve Avesnes	g.M.M.
	9/5/18		Decided to move unit to Aubigny. Sent Lorries to collect evening stores to Aubigny. Viewed Aubigny in morning to arrange details with A.G. 57 C.C. Stn. Tents moved, pitched. Visited Hauve Avesnes again and drew stores.	g.M.M.
	10/5/18		Unit marched at 3pm from Frevent Leppers to A.D. Stn. Aubigny and equipped wards same evening. Went to Manueil in morning to see A.D.M.S. re A.D.M.S. wards. Hospital now open for patients.	g.M.M.
	11/5/18		Quarter Master arranging for clean clothing for the baths. G.O.C. 3rd division invited Rest Station.	g.M.M.

WAR DIARY
INTELLIGENCE SUMMARY

Army Form C. 2118.

Vol. 37 (V)

72nd Infantry Brigade H.Q.
A.A.M.C.T.

Place	Date	Hour	Summary of Events and Information	Remarks and references to Appendices
Field	12/5/18		Sent transport to Marceul at Carieul, took horses, &c.	
			A.D.M.S. called in afternoon and discussed question of opening officers' ward.	9mm
	13/5/18		Heavy rain all day. Called at A.D.M.S. in morning re opening of officers' ward. Then visited Mat. Sec. to see O.C. as to riveted tours for sending patients to Rest Station. Orders sickbeds for hospital. Military medal awarded for gallantry between 21st & 23rd March to No. 20846 Pte Patterson, A.S. A.D.M.S. Div. Amm. visited Rest Station along with A.D.M.S. 51 Div.	9mm
	14/5/18		Coys and A.D.M.S 51 Division	9mm
	15/5/18		Capt Thompson attached to 1/3 43 Forces for temporary duty.	9mm
	16/5/18		Officers' ward (key beds) now equipped. Cipher outside wards progressing favourably.	9mm
	17/5/18		Attended conference at A.D.M.S. office concerning conformity of training of divisional regt. or wagons. Accompanied A.D.M.S to Recincourt to see deep dugouts which were excavated by R.E. Referred to Hd Qrs.	9mm

Army Form C. 2118.

WAR DIARY
of
INTELLIGENCE SUMMARY.
(Erase heading not required.)

78 Field Ambulance R.A.M.C.T.

Vol. 27 (V)

Instructions regarding War Diaries and Intelligence Summaries are contained in F. S. Regs., Part II. and the Staff Manual respectively. Title pages will be prepared in manuscript.

Place	Date	Hour	Summary of Events and Information	Remarks and references to Appendices
Field	17/5/18		Sergt Mieire and 8 men detailed to proceed to Rocliincourt and act as holding party on Dugouts. There Inspection of transport in afternoon. Weather now very hot	5pm
	18/5/18		Commence preparations for inter ambulance transport competition which is to take place on 26th. No. 508349 Sergt Cook T. awarded M.M. for gallantry between 21st Feb. & March 18.	9pm
	19/5/18		Go to Maroeuil in morning to see A.D.M.S. who is not in. Return via Ecurie meet him at 3p H.Q. Arras. He accompanies me to Aubigny and inspects the Rest Station. Conferred with O.C. 1/3 & 3/1 H.F. Amb regarding wagon marking. A party of 25 O.R. proceeded to report to Major Spurcher 1/3 H.F. Amb for temporary duty.	9pm
	20/5/18		Capt Browne detailed as M.O.i/c. Overseeing Hospital Avenue & Cross. Painting of wagons being proceeded with.	9pm
	20/5/18		Concert Party gave performance in open air in evening. Hon. Director A.D.M.S. 1st Corps. A.D.M.S. XIII Corps visited Rest Station and expressed satisfaction with arrangements.	9pm

WAR DIARY
INTELLIGENCE SUMMARY

Army Form C. 2118.

Place	Date	Hour	Summary of Events and Information	Remarks and references to Appendices
Suez	23/5/18		In afternoon I conferred with O.C. 1/3 R.Sp. D.O. having arranged on general training for personnel. Lieut Chiech detailed for temp duty with 57 C.G.Spn.	
	24/5/18		By order of A.D.M.S. I proceeded to Ecrapa recrement in afternoon to inspect and report on Jacobs disinfector in use there.	
	25/5/18		Commenced bombing in neighborhood last night. Extract from Force Gazette supplement of 22/5/18 — "Immediate Rewards conferred upon the following officers for gallantry between 15.9.43 & 9.4.18. Military Cross. A/Major A.G. Wallace, M.B.	
	26/5/18		O.N.G.M. No M/405398 Pte Keighmore, N.M. Det. A conference was held at H.d. Qrs. between Vanguard of Force Amoda (one among myself one R.S. engineer also understood from each). This went over point in all three exercises	
	29/5/18		W.O.s N.C.O.s XVII Corps called in afternoon. Sen N.C.O.s sent to attend course of Instruction at 2nd Army School opened with G.O.G. 57 Division in evening.	
	30/5/18		N.C.O. detailed to attend course of Disinfection at XVII Corps Gas School	

Army Form C. 2118.

WAR DIARY
or
INTELLIGENCE SUMMARY.
(Erase heading not required.)

1/2nd Highland Field Ambulance R.A.M.C.T.

Vol 37 (VI)

Place	Date	Hour	Summary of Events and Information	Remarks and references to Appendices
Field	30/5/18		Called at A.D.M.S. office in morning. Order received for Capt Browne to report for duty to A.D.M.S. 51st Divn. Capt Browne relieved Capt Browne at Detention Hospital.	JMM
	31/5/18		A.D.M.S. visited Red Station in afternoon.	JMM
			Note. The health of the unit during month has been excellent due in great measure to the fine weather.	

George W. Miller
LIEUT. COL., R.A.M.C., T.F.
O.C. 1/2nd HIGHLAND FIELD AMBULANCE

[Stamp: 1/2ND HIGHLAND FIELD AMBULANCE 7 JUN. 1918 R.A.M.C. (T.) B.E.F.]

140/30 76.

War Nect. 9.0.

June 1918

COMMITTEE FOR
MEDICAL HISTORY
Date 7 AUG 1918

WAR DIARY
INTELLIGENCE SUMMARY

Army Form C.2118.

Vol 38 (1)

1/2 W.J. Brew
R.A.M.C.T.

Place	Date	Hour	Summary of Events and Information	Remarks and references to Appendices
AUBIGNY.	1/5/18		Working 57 O.W. Fus. Station at Aubigny accomodating 200 patients	
	5/6/18		7 O.R. awaiting O.R. reported for duty from A.D.M.S.	
	8/6/18		No 303003 Pte M. J. Brown awarded D.C.M. for distinguished service in the field	
	11/6/18		Capt Moore reported for temporary duty to O.C. 1/3 H. D. R.M.C.	
			10 O.R. reported to O.C. 1/3 H. D. R.M.C. on recpt of similar number of O.R. of this unit.	
	12/6/18		Lieut W.P. Phillip & 2 N.C.O.s proceeded for course at Gen. Army School of Instruction	
			Capt Thompson received Field Orders at 57 C.C. Sta.	
	13/6/18		Horse Marquee was struck by morning shell was destroyed by fire this evening.	
			Court of Enquiry held on destruction of marquee by fire.	
	17/6/18		Capt Moore returned from 1/3 H. D. R.M.C.	
	15/6/18		O.R. relieved service No. attached to 1/3 H. D. R.M.C.	
			10 O.R. proceeded on leave to U.K.	
	17/6/18		Lieut Col. J.W. Miles proceeded on leave	
			Major Washbrook assumed Entry Command of unit	
	27/6/18		Lt. W.P. Phillip & 2 O.R. returned from Gen. Army School of Instn.	
	29/6/18		Lt. W.P. Phillip relieved Capt Thompson at 57 C.C. Sta.	
			Capt Thompson returned to unit.	

Army Form C. 2118.

WAR DIARY
or
INTELLIGENCE SUMMARY.

(Erase heading not required.)

Vol 38 (11)

Instructions regarding War Diaries and Intelligence Summaries are contained in F. S. Regs., Part II. and the Staff Manual respectively. Title pages will be prepared in manuscript.

Place	Date	Hour	Summary of Events and Information	Remarks and references to Appendices
Aveluy	24/6/18		Orders received at 5 p.m. to be taken over by Capt. Thompson and proceeded as temporary M.O. I/c. R9a.25.5 v 25.6. Brigaded	Grandchamp 24/6
	30/6/18		Owing to presence of A.W.C. in Division increased hospital accommodation had to be provided during month.	Maq. bit Maqui
			Accommodation for 500 available at this date.	

J McGrish
Major, R.A.M.C. T.
1/3rd HIGHLAND FIELD AMBULANCE.

[Stamp: 1/3 HIGHLAND FIELD AMBULANCE, 1 JUL 1918, R.A.M.C. (T) B.E.F.]

149/3131.

Army Form C. 2118.

WAR DIARY
of
INTELLIGENCE SUMMARY.

(Erase heading not required.) 1/2 H.F. A/33 R.A.M.C.T.

Vol 39 (1)

Instructions regarding War Diaries and Intelligence Summaries are contained in F. S. Regs., Part II. and the Staff Manual respectively. Title pages will be prepared in manuscript.

Place	Date	Hour	Summary of Events and Information	Remarks and references to Appendices
AUBIGNY	1/4/18		Working Divisions Rest Station at AUBIGNY. Lieut Philip returned to unit for duty.	A/32 3 gmm
	5/4/18		Lieut. Philip received Capt. Thompson at 57 C.C.Stn. Major Mackintosh proceeded on leave.	gmm
	6/4/18		Major Wallace assumed temporary command of unit.	gmm
	7/4/18		Lt.Col. Miller returned from leave & took over command of unit. Epidemic of PUO dying down considerably.	gmm
	8/4/18		A.D.M.S. called in afternoon	gmm
	9/4/18		Division commander being received from line.	gmm
	10/4/18		Orders received not to evacuate any cases unless condition has moved. Received message from A.D.M.S. XVII Corps asking how many cases could be admitted from 56 Division as they were overcrowded. Replied 50. 57 Cases actually sent.	gmm
	11/4/18		Heavy thunder showers during day. Col Weston A.A. & Q.M.G. of Division called before leaving for home introduced Col Fitzgerald new A.A. & Q.M.G. Had conversation with A.D.M.S. XVII Corps at midday with reference to handing over of permanent structures on rest Stn site. Major Wallace proceeded on leave.	gmm
	13/4/18		Called at R.O.M.S. at POELLECOURT to enquire as to the preservity of the patients	gmm

Army Form C. 2118.

WAR DIARY
of
INTELLIGENCE SUMMARY.
(Erase heading not required.) 2/1 F.A. R.A.M.C.T

Vol 39 (11)

Instructions regarding War Diaries and Intelligence Summaries are contained in F. S. Regs., Part II. and the Staff Manual respectively. Title pages will be prepared in manuscript.

Place	Date	Hour	Summary of Events and Information	Remarks and references to Appendices
AUBIGNY	12/7/18		Visited Divisional Reception Camp at TINCQUES and arranged to send 50 patients this afternoon.	R.M.M.
	13/7/18		Discharged 101 patients to duty. Drew up programme for interior training. Warning order received at 7pm for immediate evacuation of divisional patients.	R.M.M.
	14/7/18		Called on A.D.M.S. and made arrangements for evacuation of all patients. This was completed during the night. Detailed arrangements arrived to evacuate at TINCQUES at 9am following day. (51st D.A.I. No 55 dated 14/7/18)	R.M.M.
			A.D.M.S. XVII Corps called in afternoon and expressed satisfaction with all that had been done. 2/Lt Gordon De Amfa took over Rest Station. Lieut Philip + Capt Thompson detailed as entraining + detraining officers respectively.	R.M.M.
	15/7/18		Reveille at 5am. Transport march off at 7.30am and proceeded at 8.30am to TINCQUES. Entrain at 12.30pm along with 1/00 Vel Section.	R.M.M.
	16/7/18		Travelled via ETAPLES, ABBEVILLE, PARIS to NOGENT sur SEINE. Detrain at 6.30pm. Start at roadside for tea + to water + feed horses. Move at 9.45pm.	R.M.M.
	17/7/18		Capt Redfern reports from Lines of Communication + hereby attached.	

D. D. & L., London, E.C. (A809) We. W1771/M.F.31 750,000 5/17 **Sch. 52** Forms/C2118/4

Army Form C. 2118.

WAR DIARY
of
INTELLIGENCE SUMMARY.
(Erase heading not required.)

VOL 39 (III)

1/2TH. F.A. R.A.M.C.T.

Instructions regarding War Diaries and Intelligence Summaries are contained in F. S. Regs., Part II. and the Staff Manual respectively. Title pages will be prepared in manuscript.

Place	Date	Hour	Summary of Events and Information	Remarks and references to Appendices
Field	17/8	1am	Stand by reveille for reck. Reveille 4am. March at 5am via ROMILLY ST JUST and ANGLURE to LA CHAPPELLE LASSON. Distance from NOGENT sur SEINE 31 kms. Arrived at 10am. Out of touch with division. Extremely hot weather.	
	18/8		A.A.Q.M.G. 11am. Called at 9pm and gave orders for following day. Reveille 4.30am. Marched at 5am via QUEUDES and SEZANNE to SOISY AU BOIS. Distance 27 miles. Arrived at 12pm. Weather rather cooler. Went to Divisional Hd Qrs in afternoon to try & arrange for French refs here to arrange for billets. Met Capt Thompson at Hd Qrs. Returned to SOISY au Bois and found lorries just arrived. 1/3 Hd Qrs also over billets. Lorries with personnel arrived in PIERRE about 9pm. Heavy bombing of surrounding district during night. Reported to A.D.M.S. at 9.30am. Division moving up rapidly. Enemy in retreat. Orders received to march tonight to CHAMPILLON.	9pm
	19/8		from SOISY au BOIS at 8pm. March at 8.30pm via EPERNAY. Arrived around CHAMPILLON at 10.30pm. Halt and HT ANS Cea J. Wait on road until midnight to get	9pm

Army Form C. 2118.

WAR DIARY
of
INTELLIGENCE SUMMARY.
(Erase heading not required.) 1/3rd H.F.A.'s R.A.M.C.

Vol 39 (N)

Instructions regarding War Diaries and Intelligence Summaries are contained in F. S. Regs., Part II. and the Staff Manual respectively. Title pages will be prepared in manuscript.

Place	Date	Hour	Summary of Events and Information	Remarks and references to Appendices
Sezanne	19/2/18		Capt Thompson detailed for duty at operating centre EPERNAY.	gmm.
	20/2/18		Occupy Dressing Station site at CHAMPILLON at 1am. ADMS called at 5am. Reveillé 7am. Equip. Main Dress Stn. Very good site with large dressing room. Accommodation of patients. A.D.M.S. XXII Corps called at 10am. Major Smith, Major Hucker & Capt Green reported for temp duty as M.O. Wounded began to arrive at 11am. Came in steadily till 5.00 evacuation. 5 Cars evacuated sick at 11am. 7 Cars at 5pm. and 2 cars at 8pm. evacuated to SEZANNE a distance of about 50 km. Main road shelled in evening. French ammunition Convoy hit by enemy shell on road about 100 yds from dressing Stn. carrying number of casualties. Collected and dressed same. 200 cases awaiting evacuation by evening. Stretchers and medical stores unobtainable during day. Carry on with what was carried by cart. Car arrived at 8pm from SEZANNE with stretchers, chocolate etc. A.D.M.S. called at 11pm.	gmm. gmm. gmm. gmm.

D. D. & L., London, E.C. (A8004) Wt. W4777/M2 31 750,000 5/17 Sch 52 Forms/C2118/4

Army Form C. 2118.

WAR DIARY
INTELLIGENCE SUMMARY.
(Erase heading not required.) 1/3H.F. Amb R.A.M.C.T.

Vol. 29 (V)

Place	Date	Hour	Summary of Events and Information	Remarks and references to Appendices
Dicel	21/7/18		Fairly quiet night. 15 Cars & one Italian lorry arrived at 6 a.m. one Car at 7 a.m. and another at 10.15 a.m. Some cases have been in Dressing Station for 24 hrs. Dressing gun gangrene.	g.m.m.
		10.15	Supply of blankets sent up to 6 R.O.T.Sta.	
		10 pm	Message received from R.O.M.S. that 42 M.A.C. evacuates at disposal of 57 Division.	
			Rode to R.O. Sta. in afternoon and saw R.O.M.S. and O.C. Dorsets. Evacuations regarding supply of stretchers.	
		5 p.m.	M.A.C. Cars now in sufficient numbers. All roads now clear by 9 p.m. Medical comforts, stretchers and blankets now available.	g.m.m.
	22/7/18		Very quiet night. Dressing Station being kept clear. Employed personnel in repairing roads and on general rarefaction which is very bad. Another quiet night.	
	23/7/18		Very quiet night. About 100 cases passed through. Division attacked again this morning. Have heavy casualties. Sent 6 M.A.C. Cars to await evacuating R.O.Sta. Now Dressing Station nearer front line. All Clear by 8 p.m. they could be evacuated. All Clear by 9 p.m. (200 wounded cases passed through)	g.m.m. g.m.m.

WAR DIARY
of
INTELLIGENCE SUMMARY.

(Erase heading not required.) 1/2 1/4 F.A. R.A.M.C.T

Army Form C. 2118.

Vol 29 (VI)

Instructions regarding War Diaries and Intelligence Summaries are continued in F. S. Regs., Part II. and the Staff Manual respectively. Title pages will be prepared in manuscript.

Place	Date	Hour	Summary of Events and Information	Remarks and references to Appendices
Sezed	23/7/18		A.D.M.S. called in evening. Situation quieter. Shewe toward evening.	4mm
	24/7/18		Very quiet last night. A.D.M.S. called early. Very quiet all day. Major Marchrush returns from leave. Capt. Hewitt kept wright reports for duty.	4mm
	25/7/18		Fair number of wounded during night. Capt wright remains for duty at M.D. the meantime. Major Marchrush proceeds today to Cachye. Collect medical stores from SEZANNE. Capt Green returns to his unit. Capt Thompson returns from opening Camp EPERNAY.	4mm
	26/7/18		No. 34 Sanitary Section arrive and are attached to this unit - Very quiet during night and all day. Sent car to SEZANNE for stores.	3mm
	27/7/18		Wireless attack again this morning. Heavy rain in evening. A.D.M.S. called at 8.30 a.m. Wounded begin to arrive at 10 a.m. Sent 50 stretchers to A.D.S. A.D. Conscn receiving check. Many casualties. Col. Collett G.H.Q. Smith called in afternoon. Received demand from A.D.M.S. for 50 stretchers. Only 12 on hand. Orders received from A.D.M.S. to move tomorrow to ST IMOGE S. C.C.S. in evening. 50 sent to M.D.S.	4mm 3/mm

100. STRETCHER Arrived

Army Form C. 2118.

Vol 39 (VII)

WAR DIARY
of
INTELLIGENCE SUMMARY.
(Erase heading not required.) 1/2 H.F.A. R.A.M.C.

Place	Date	Hour	Summary of Events and Information	Remarks and references to Appendices
Fresse	27/7/18		Proceeded there along with Q.M. D.M. to see accommodation. Capt. Thompson and party go up tonight to prepare these sites.	5mm.
	28/7/18		Very quiet afternoon and evening. Very heavy rain. Reveille 5:30 a.m. Capt. Melvin & evacuating Stations Party leave at 6 a.m. New N.O. to be ready for patients at 7:30 a.m. Remainder of unit march from CHATILLON at 7:45 a.m. and arrive at ST IMOGES at 8:30 a.m. Arrange system of evacuation and start rendering squads cleaning up march to heaps. Levels very bad. Division attacks again this morning. Cases coming in by 9:30 a.m. Hospital becoming occupied by French troops. Arrange with Town Major to have them all cleared afternoon. Busy all afternoon and evening. A.D.M.S. seems very short and these evacuated, also Thomas's service.	2mm.
	29/7/18		Very busy all night. 2 rooms. G.H.Q. South along with Official Historian called and looked round. D. Evening Star. at 6 p.m. Director General called and inspected one wing Chateau	5mm.

Army Form C. 2118.

WAR DIARY
of
INTELLIGENCE SUMMARY.
(Erase heading not required.)

Vol X9 (VIII)

/3H.F.A.R.A.M.C.T

Instructions regarding War Diaries and Intelligence Summaries are contained in F. S. Regs., Part II. and the Staff Manual respectively. Title pages will be prepared in manuscript.

Place	Date	Hour	Summary of Events and Information	Remarks and references to Appendices
Field	29/7/18		Q.M. went to SEZANNE and drew supply of A.T. Serum also Thomas Splints.	8 p.m.
	30/7/18		Very quiet last night. Quantity of rockets now carried and fired not so numerous. Went to NANTEUIL in evening and saw A.D.M.S. about relief. Orders arrived in evening for entraining of division. Capt Wright detailed to 48 C.C.She. Capt Thompson detailed to 14 Gnl Hghtn.	8 p.m.
	31/7/18		A.D.M.S. called in morning. Major Thirsk to remain with this unit in meantime. Capt Roy reported for duty. Arranged to return all surplus stores, blankets &c. to 48 C.C.She. Capt Melvin & Capt Roy detailed as entraining & detraining medical officers respectively. Visited 1/3 3rd Ambce to arrange about stretchers & blankets. Major Joseph returned to 1/3 3rd Ambce Orders received to entrain at AVIZES at 8 p.m. on 31st August. Bearer cars returned from forward area at 8 p.m. Stokes aircraft bombed heavily all night. At midnight a convoy of bearer cars opposite hospital carrying several casualties to French troops disabled there.	8 p.m. 8 p.m.

Army Form C. 2118.

Vol 39 (IX)

WAR DIARY
or
INTELLIGENCE SUMMARY.
(Erase heading not required.) 1/2 H.F.A. R.A.M.C.T

Instructions regarding War Diaries and Intelligence Summaries are contained in F. S. Regs., Part II. and the Staff Manual respectively. Title pages will be prepared in manuscript.

Place	Date	Hour	Summary of Events and Information	Remarks and references to Appendices
Zuel	31/3/18		Orders received to march successively to CRAMANT area	gmm
			Honoured	
			Number of wounded passed through Main Dress Stn for period 30/3/18 to 31/3/18.	
			Officers 101	
			O.R. 1466.	
			Note. During stay in South Area there was a prevalence of diarrhoea throughout the unit which was probably due to the large number of flies. Casualties were few only 5 bearers being wounded, one of whom died later from gas poisoning	gmm

George W. Miller
LIEUT. COL., R.A.M.C., T.F.
O.C. 1/2nd HIGHLAND FIELD AMBULANCE

16/3700.

1/2nd Nyh. + a.

Aug. 1918.

(6202) W 11186/M1151 350,000 12/16 McA. & W., Ltd. (Est. 781) Forms/W 3091/3.   Army Form W. 3091.

Cover for Documents.

Nature of Enclosures.

Notes, or Letters written.

Volume No. _____

BRITISH SALONIKA FORCE

WAR DIARY.

Medical Units,   26th Division.

Vol. No.	Unit	PERIOD From	To
30.	A.D.M.S.	1.4.18.	30.4.18.
28.	78th Fld. Amb.	"	"
29.	79th " "	"	"
28.	80th " "	"	"
19.	43rd Sanitary Section.	"	"

A.P. & S.D., Alex./No. 752/8:5:17/3000 (50041G/53) W. M. & Co.

WAR DIARY of 1/2nd Highland Field Ambulance, Army Form C. 2118.
R.A.M.C. T.F.
or
INTELLIGENCE SUMMARY. Vol. 40 Page 1.

(Erase heading not required.)

Instructions regarding War Diaries and Intelligence Summaries are contained in F.S. Regs., Part II. and the Staff Manual respectively. Title pages will be prepared in manuscript.

Place	Date	Hour	Summary of Events and Information	Remarks and references to Appendices
Field. ST. IMOGES.	1/8/18.		Packed up hospital in morning and marched at 10 a.m. from ST. IMOGES to CRAMMONT, via EPERNAY. Arrived at 3-30 p.m. The following American Medical Officers joined the unit for duty, viz:- Lieut. Finch, P. " Glass, T.W. " Ashby, G.M. " Robinson, J.W. Sent note to MT Coy. to arrange for cars for collection of sick on the 2nd inst. Called at H.Q. 152 Inf. Bde. at OGER in evening. Received altered time for entraining. Reported to A.D.M.S. at CRAMMONT and returned to H.Q.	mm
	2/8/18.		Very hot day. Went to AVIZES to interview French Area Commandant and arrange about holding billets until following day. Cars report to M.T. Coy. EPERNAY, in forenoon and return to unit, remaining there for evacuation of sick till 8 pm. when they proceeded for entraining. Lieut. Glass relieved Major Melvin as entraining officer at EPERNAY. Major Hunter returns to 1/3rd Highland Field Ambulance. Billeting party of 3 O.R. proceed to new area.	mm
	3/8/18.		Réveille at 4-30a.m. Unit marches at 6 a.m. to AVIZES for entrainment. S.M. Gosling sick. Entraining finished at 10-30 a.m. Train proceeds up to time.	mm
	4/8/18.		Journeyed all day and arrived at PERNES at 8 pm. Two lorries conveyed part of unit; remainder marched at 9 p.m. after watering and feeding horses, to CAMBLIGNEUL (13 miles).	mm
	5/8/18.		Arrived at CAMBLIGNEUL at 2 am. Major Wallace who had returned from leave, had billets arranged. Called at A.D.M.S. at midday regarding Medical Arrangements. Visited Medical Officers of 152 Inf. Bde. and gave them A.D.M.S. instructions. Captain Roy reported for duty from detraining station. Lieuts. Robinson and Ashby detailed to 2/1st High. Field Ambulance. Serjt-Major Gosling evacuated to C.C.S. Heavy rain all day.	mm
	6/8/18.		A.D.M.S. called and inspected billets. Opened Brigade Hospital with 20 beds. Made investigations/	mm

Page 2.

WAR DIARY of 1/2nd Highland Field Ambulance,
R.A.M.C. T.F.
Vol. 40 page 2.

INTELLIGENCE SUMMARY.

Place	Date	Hour	Summary of Events and Information	Remarks and references to Appendices
FIELD. GAMBLIGNEUL.	6/8/18		Made investigations concerning Wounded after CHAMPAGNE battle, arising out of question by D.D.M.S. as to improvised splints etc. Reported result to A.D.M.S.	
	7/8/18.		Sanitation work around hospital.	
	8/8/18.		Sent in programme of intensive training. Called at 53 C.C.S. to see Serjt-Major.	
	9/8/18.		Went to distribution of remounts in morning. Commenced training, copy of Training Scheme attached.	
	10/8/18.		G.O.C. Division called in morning. Lieut. Glass detailed to attend First Army School of instruction along with 2 men. Capt. Roy detailed as temp. M.O. i/c. 208 Squadron, R.A.F. A.D.M.S. called in evening.	
	11/8/18.		Sent indent for material to repair huts, and for making of trestles. Attended conference at A.D.M.S. Office in afternoon.	
	12/8/18.		Lieut. Lurier, M.R.C. U.S. reported for duty. Received Warning order for move the following day. Replied to note regarding German M.Os. not being allowed to attend to German Wounded during ARRAS Battle, April-May 1917. Statements without foundation. Arranged to get motor lorry for surplus equipment. Lieut. Finch detailed as M.O. i/c. 1/4th Sea. Highrs in relief of Capt. Moore. Orders to march to MAROEUIL and take over from 1/2nd Low. F. Amb. on 14th received.	
	13/8/18.		Orders cancelled. Called on A.D.M.S. at 8.30 a.m. for information and again in afternoon. M.T. Officers from G.H.Q. inspected Motor Ambulances. Authority granted by G.O.C. 51st High. Division to Capt. Melvin to wear the badges of Major whilst commanding a Section of this Ambulance.	
	14/8/18.		Along with A.D.M.S. 51st High. Div. called on D.D.M.S. XVII Corps and A.Ds.M.S. 52nd and 57th Divisions.	

Page 3. Vol.40. Army Form C. 2118.

WAR DIARY of 1/2nd High. Field Ambulance, R.A.M.C. T.F.

INTELLIGENCE SUMMARY

Place	Date	Hour	Summary of Events and Information	Remarks and references to Appendices
	15/8/18 Continued.		Divisions regarding reliefs. 1/2nd High. Field Ambulance to go to ST. CATHARINE. 19 On return detailed bearers to Battalions of 154 Bde. Detailed Lieut.Lurier and 1& O.R. to take over CHANTECLER POST and CUTTING (B.27.a.4-7). Sheet 51.B. Major Mallace accompanies him to make arrangements. Col. Leach 1/1st Low. F. Amb. called in evening regarding taking over of site presently occupied by this unit.	smit
	16/8/18.		Went with Major Mallace to MAROEUIL at 10 a.m., met A.D.M.S. there and went on to ST. CATHARINE, then visited CHANTECLER POST. Made arrangements as to rationing of men here, also for evacuation of patients for tonight. Returned to MAROEUIL and then to CAMBLIGNEUL. In afternoon Lieut. Johnston and Q.M.S. Brown went to CHANTECLER with stores and rations. A car was stationed at Main Dressing Station for duty.	smit
	17/8/18.		Went with Major Mallace to ST. CATHARINE and along with Capt. Loudon 3/2nd West Lancs. Field visited POINT DU JOUR, GAM VALLEY and L'ABBAYETTE, and returned to ST. CATHARINE. Move of unit postponed for 24 hours. Reported to A.D.M.S. at MAROEUIL and returned to CAMBLIGNEUL. Major Mallace to L'ABBAYETTE to take over Adv. Dress. Station there. This party remained overnight at Main Dressing Station, ST. CATHARINE.	smit
	18/8/18		Went with car at 9 a.m. to ST. CATHARINE, called at Main Dressing Station and picked up stores for CHANTECLER ; walked on with Lieut. Lurier to CUTTING POST. Visited R.A.P. 1/4 Sea. Highrs. at GUN PITS. Called at 154 Inf. Bde. HQ. and saw Brigadier and Staff Captain. Returned to Main Dressing Station. Called at A.D.M.S. office in afternoon and while there saw A.D.M.S. 57th Div. Arranged with him to take over Railway Triangle Post (H.19.b.3-1. Sheet 51 B.) and other posts on South side of SCARPE until relief of Bde. belonging to 57th Div. Returned to CAMBLIGNEUL. Extra bearers from 1/3rd High. Field Amb. reported for duty. Sent Q.M.S. Gregory (A.S.C. M.T.) to Main Dressing Station ST. CATHARINE to arrange car service in Forward Area. Major Mallace proceeded to A.D.S. L'ABBAYETTE. Capt. Moore with advance party proceeded to Main Dress. Station, ST. CATHARINE. Heavily bombed last night. Fourteen horses killed and 12 wounded.	smit
	19/8/18.		Reveille at 5 a.m. Transport move at 7 a.m. under Lieut. Johnston. Major Melvin accompanied me to Main Dressing Station, ST. CATHARINE. Capt. Gorrie/	smit

Army Form C. 2118.

WAR DIARY of 1/2nd High. Field Ambulance,
R.A.M.C. T.F.
Vol. 40 page 4.

INTELLIGENCE SUMMARY
or
(Erase heading not required.)

Instructions regarding War Diaries and Intelligence Summaries are contained in F.S. Regs., Part II. and the Staff Manual respectively. Title pages will be prepared in manuscript.

Place	Date	Hour	Summary of Events and Information	Remarks and references to Appendices
	19/8/18.		Cap. Gorrie 1/3rd High. Field Ambce. reported for temp. duty at Main Dress. Station. Capt. Moore proceeded to L'ABBAYETTE in afternoon. Transport arrived at 10-30a.m. and un-loaded all wagons at M.D.S. thereafter proceeding to horse lines at ANZIM POST. 30 bearers arrived from 1/3rd High. Field Ambce. reported last night for RAILWAY TRIANGLE POST. Accompanied A.D.M.S. to L'ABBAYETTE in afternoon. Returned to ST. CATHARINE and attended conference at A.D.M.S. Office. Saw Major Fox D.A. & Q.M.G. about loss of horses and provision of remounts Saw Major Wallace 20 extra bearers and extra carss and wheeled stretcher carriers. Some activity expected tomorrow. Sent Major Wallace 20 extra bearers and extra carss and wheeled stretcher carriers.	gmm
	20/8/18.		Visited Horse lines in morning and gave directions regarding protection against bombing, repair of latrines etc. Visited CHANTECLER POST. Arranged to recall bearers from reserve battalions. Visited Quarry POST and RAILWAY TRIANGLE, and arranged to take over new dug-out at the latter for the reserve bearers there. Visited A.D.S. L'ABBAYETTE. Went to 152nd Inf. Bde. H.Q. and saw Brigadier. Thereafter returned to Main Dressing Station. Went to Divisional H.Q. in afternoon regarding relief of bearers South of SCARPE.	mmb
	21/8/18.		Heavy barrage at day-break on this front. Visited CHANTECLER at 6 a.m., and found all quiet. Went on to L'ABBAYETTE: about 20 cases had passed through Dressing Station there. Visited QUARRY POST and 152 Bde. H.Q. on return journey. Bearers at RAILWAY TRIANGLE relieved, with exception of eight. Major Hunter, 1/3rd High. Field Ambulance reported for duty. A.D.M.S. called in evening. Weather very hot.	mmb
	22/8/18.		Visited L'ABBAYETTE at 10 a.m. and returned via BLANGY and ARRAS GUNNERS' POSTS. Called on A.D.M.S. at MAROEUIL in afternoon, and then D.A.D.O.S. and O.C. 51st M.V.S. at AGNEZ-LES-DUISANS. An officer from Life Guards M.G. Batn. called in evening about taking over from Brigade South of SCARPE. No medical arrangements. Sent N.C.O. to RAILWAY TRIANGLE to take charge there. Large number of gassed cases admitted during the day. 23/8/18./ Very hot day.	gmm

WAR DIARY of 1/2nd Highland Field Ambulance,
R.A.M.C.T.F. Vol. 40 Page 5.

or
INTELLIGENCE SUMMARY.
(Erase heading not required.)

Army Form C.2118

Place	Date	Hour	Summary of Events and Information	Remarks and references to Appendices
Field.	23/8/18.		Went to CHANTECLER in morning, and walked on to CUTTING POST and GULLY R.A.P. (1/7th Arg.& Suthd. Highrs.). On return FROM found G.H.Q. M.T. Officers again examining cars. A large number of gassed cases continued to come in. Went to H.Q. in afternoon to see A.D.M.S. about disposal of gassed clothing.	
	24/8/18.		Along with Major Hunter, I visited A.D.S. and went round R.A.Ps. with him and Major Wallace. Major Hunter relieved Major Wallace at A.D.S. Relief of bearers arranged for R.A.Ps. In afternoon visited A.D.M.S. and went with him to 2/1st High Field Ambulance at AGNEZ-LES-DUISANS. Arranged for extra bearers to be sent up. Capt. Roy and Lieut. Glass returned to unit. Capt. Gorrie returns to 1/3rd High. Field Ambulance. Major Wallace proceeded to A.D.M.S. Office in temp. relief of D.A.D.M.S. A.D.M.S. called at 10 a.m. and met D.D.M.S. Canadian Corps. Medical arrangements completed for the Battle tomorrow.	
	25/8/18.		Large number of gassed cases came in during the day. Over a hundred from 1/6th Gord. Hrs. At 6 p.m. changed from M.D.S. to A.D.S. ST. CATHARINE. Sent wagons to 2/1st High. Field Ambce. for extra stretchers (125) and blankets (200) 40 bearers arrived from 2/1st H.F.A. in evening. Sent up 40 stretchers and 50 blankets each, to CHANTECLER and L'ABBAYETTE Posts at night. About 8 p.m. visited CHANTECLER, thence to H.Qrs. of the three Inf. Bdes. and then to L'ABBAYETTE. Heavy rain with thunder. Returned to A.D.S. at midnight. TRIANGLE POST not yet relieved. Telephoned A.D.M.S. at 1-30 a.m. (26th).	
	26/8/18.		Barrage fire at 4-30 a.m. Visited L'ABBAYETTE with A.D.M.S. D.D.M.S. Canadian Corps called in afternoon and gave instructions for party to be withdrawn from RAILWAY TRIANGLE. Visited CHANTECLER POST in afternoon and found all quiet. Proceeded from there to 152 and 153 Inf. Bde. H.Q. They are moving forward to CAM VALLEY and EFFIE post respectively. Went on to QUARRY POST and L'ABBAYETTE. Along with Major Hunter I went to FAMPOUX and selected site for Car Collecting Post. Road very much blocked by fallen trees and trenches, but being cleared by pioneers. Major Hunter sent N.C.O. and 4 men to open Collecting Post and arranged to run cars as soon as road is clear. Returned to ST. CATHARINE and reported to A.D.M.S. by telephone. D.D.G.M.S./	

Army Form C. 2118.

Instructions regarding War Diaries and Intelligence
Summaries are contained in F.S. Regs., Part II.
and the Staff Manual respectively. Title pages
will be prepared in manuscript.

WAR DIARY of 1/2nd High. Field Ambulance.

or
INTELLIGENCE SUMMARY.

Vol. 40. page 6.

(Erase heading not required.)

Place	Date	Hour	Summary of Events and Information	Remarks and references to Appendices
Field.	26/8/18.		D.D.G.M.S. called in forenoon. D.D.M.S. Can. Corps and A.D.M.S. Division called at teatime and discussed Medical arrangements. At 5 p.m. A.D.S. again changed to M.D.S. 2/1st High. Field Ambulance being Div. Rest Station.	nil
	27/8/18.		A.D.M.S. called at 9 am. and I accompanied him to Div. H.Q. at BLANGY and afterwards to L'ABBAY L'ABBAYETTE and FAMPOUX. Returned to QUARRY POST, made arrangements for feeding walking Wounded there, thence to POINT DU JOUR to arrange for ambulance cars to run to that post, and on to CHANTECLER and 154 Inf. Bde. H.Q. Instructed Lieut. LURIER to evacuate CHANTECLER POST leaving a small holding party, and to proceed to POINT DU JOUR as M.O. i/c. there. Arranged for cars to be sent to move his equipment. Q.M.S. proceeds to POINT DU JOUR to superintend evacuation of stores. Visited L'ABBAYETTE and 152nd Inf. Bde. H.Q. in evening and thence to POINT DU JOUR and 153 Inf. Bde. H.Q. Report in evening to A.D.M.S concerning position of R.A.Ps.	nil
	28/8/18.		A.D.M.S. called in morning. I then went with Q.Master to POINT DU JOUR and L'ABBAYETTE. Afterwards proceeding with Major Hunter to FAMPOUX, to reconnoitre road beyond that to ONE ARCHED BRIDGE, (H.18 b.2.1.). Road impossible at present. Visited 152 Inf. Bde. at CAM VALLEY and told them of my intention to run cars to the BRIDGE as soon as the road became available. M.O. at CUTTING POST handed over to party of 8th Div. and returned to "M.D.S." with party. Reported to A.D.M.S. with notes of positions of R.A.Ps. A.D.M.S. called in afternoon, and arranged to hold up sick at M.D.S. for one night to allow D.R.S. to move from AGNEZ-LES-DUISA'S to ECOIVRES. Capt. Moore taken on strength of unit and Lieut. Finch posted to 1/4th Sea. Highrs in his place.	nil
	29/8/18.		Detailed Lieut. Glass to proceed to 1/5 Sea. Highrs. in relief of Lieut. McGregor. Went with A.D.M.S. to L'ABBAYETTE, taking Capt. Roy to relieve Major Hunter. Called at POINT DU JOUR and left instructions for Lieut. Lurier to proceed to L'ABBAYETTE for duty, and send surplus bearers back to ST. CATHARINE. 153 Inf. Bde. now relieved by 154 Bde. Went on to FAMPOUX with Capt. Roy and A.D.M.S. and met Brigadier 152nd Inf. Bde. there. In afternoon visited POINT DU JOUR and L'ABBAYETTE. Went with Capt. Roy to arrange for Car Collecting Post belond FAMPOUX. Selected the site at SANDPITS (H.18. a.2.4.) Good d-outs available but very dirty. Sent N.C.O. and 4 men to clean up and remain there.	nil
	30/8/18.		A.D.M.S. called.	

Army Form C. 2118.

WAR DIARY of 1/2nd High. Field Ambulance, R.A.M.C. T.F.
or
INTELLIGENCE SUMMARY. Vol. 40 page 7.
(Erase heading not required.)

Instructions regarding War Diaries and Intelligence Summaries are contained in F. S. Regs., Part II. and the Staff Manual respectively. Title pages will be prepared in manuscript.

Place	Date	Hour	Summary of Events and Information	Remarks and references to Appendices
	30/8/18.		A.D.M.S. called in the morning and I accompanied him to FAMPOUX, then to SANDPITS Collecting Post. Proceed along CHEMICAL WORKS ROAD to I.13.a.1.1. to find site for Collecting Post. Found dug out in Quarry which was heavily shelled just after we left. As this road did not serve either Bde. well, we judged it unsuitable. Returned to ONE ARCH BRIDGE and visited 1/4th Gord. Highrs. Aid Post. Detailed R.A.M.C. working party to repair road from FAMPOUX to BRIDGE and render it practicable for cars. This was completed by evening. *[an service rendu]*	*initl.*
	31/8/18.		Visited QUARRY POST with Q.M.S. Brown, then proceede to L'ABBAYETTE. Went with Capt. Roy to ROEUX to reconnoitre state of road. Quite hopeless for cars beyond ONE ARCH BRIDGE. Proceeded again up road towards RAILWAY CROSS ROADS at I.13.a.0.3. but were stopped by shelling. Met A.D.M.S. at ST. CATHARINE on return. Under authority granted by His Majesty The King, the XXII Corps Commander awarded the following decorations for gallantry displayed between 20th and 31st July,1918, Bar to Military Medal. 56157. Pte. Boyd, W. Military Medal. 5302. Pte. Hayter, J.W. 7656. Pte. Jordan, F.G. 303148. " Simpson, S. 75632. " Jones, G. 303132. " Leith, W.P. 9919. " Greenwood, F. 303113. " Jackson, B. 51133. " Locock, H. --- NOTE. During occupation of Main Dressing Station, casualties on the whole have been very light about an average of 50 Wounded a day. The heaviest days were due to gas, and limited to 1/6th Gord. Highrs. and 1/5th Sea. Highrs., each losing about 100 men from this cause while in succession holding the same section of the line.	*initl.* *initl.* *initl.*

George W. Miller
Lieut-Col.,
C... 1/2nd Highland Field Ambulance, R.A.M.C. T.F.

1/2nd Highland Field Ambulance, R.A.M.C. T.F.

PROGRAMME OF REST TRAINING.

FIRST DAY.

9 to 10 a.m. — Physical Drill.

10-15 to
11-15 a.m. — Lecture — The Treatment of Fractures in Adv. and Main
Dressing Stations. The application of Thomas'
and other special splints.

11-30 to
12-30. — Anti-gas Instruction and Drill — Different types of Gas.
Box-Respirators — How to detect faults.
How to apply.
Marching and working with them on.

2 to 3 p.m. — Medical Bhore Cart and Wagon — Checking Equipment.
Rapid Loading and unloading.

Second Day.

9 to 10 a.m. — Physical Drill.

10-15 to
11-15. — Lecture — The Treatment of Wounds and Haemorrhage in Adv.
and Main Dressing Stations.
Preparation and Sterilisation of Dressings.
Preparation and Use of Antiseptic Solutions.

11-30 to
12-30. — Loading and Unloading of Ambulance Cars.
Special attention to be paid to the careful handling of
patients.

2 to 3 p.m. — Squad Drill.

THIRD DAY.

9 to 10 a.m. — Physical Drill.

10-15 to
11-15. — Lecture — Nursing Duties — Observation of Cases.
Day and Night Reports. Treatment of Feverish
patients. Anti-shock Measures. Careful blanketing
Hot Drinks. Hot-air Baths etc.

11-30 to
12-30. — Preparation and Equipment of Adv. Dressing Station.

2 to 3 p.m. — Construction of Improvised Shelters. Preparation of Hot
Drinks, Sandwiches etc.

FOURTH DAY./

2.

FOURTH DAY.
9 to 10a.m.   Physical Drill.
10-15 to
 11-15.   Lecture. — Water Duties. Their Importance in prevention
          of disease. How water is contaminated.
          Water-borne Diseases. Prophylaxis, Inocul-
          ation. Safe Water supply. How obtained.
          Field Purification. Water Carts.

11-30 to
 12-30.   Supply and Transport of (a) Medical Stores, (b) Water,
          (c) Rations in Battle.
          Improvisation of Packsaddles.
2 to 5 p.m.   Loading and Unloading. Same

FIFTH DAY.
9 to 10 a.m.   Physical Drill.
10-15 to
 11-15.   Lecture. — Sanitation in the Field.
          (1) On the March. (2) In Camp and Billets.
          Cookhouses. Ablution Benches. Soak Pits
          and Grease Traps. Incinerators.
          Latrines (1) Deep. (2) Bucket.

11-30 to
 12-30.   Stretcher Drill. Field Practices.
2 to 5 p.m.   Squad Drill.

SIXTH DAY.
9 to 10 a.m.   Physical Drill.
10-15 to
 11-15.   Lecture. — Ambulance Work in Open and Semi-open Warfare.
          Lessons from Recent Battles. Adv. Dressing
          Stations in Advance and Retreat.
          Importance of Keeping Touch.

11-30 to
 12-30.   Route March — Full Marching Order. March Discipline to
          be strictly observed.
2 to 5p.m.   Water Duties (Practical) Care of Water Cart. Explanation
          of parts. Practical illustration of Working.

SEVENTH DAY.
PRACTICAL SCHEME.   Two Officers and Adv. Dressing Station Party and
          Bearers will be sent at short notice to open an
          Adv. Dressing Station and get touch with R.A.Ps.of
          a Brigade that has been hurriedly rushed into the
          Line.
          This will be carried out by different officers and
          men on different days of the week, and will be
          made as practical as possible.

N.B. Instruction will be given to N.C.Os. in Map Reading and Water-
     Testing at times to be selected.

14/3259.

1/2t. Hugh. F. A.

Sep. 1918.

WAR DIARY or **INTELLIGENCE SUMMARY**

1/2nd Highland Field Ambulance, R.A.M.C., T.F.

Vol. 41. Page 1.

Army Form C. 2118.

Place	Date	Hour	Summary of Events and Information	Remarks and references to Appendices
St. CATHERINE.	1/9/18.		Along with A.D.M.S. I visited A.D.S. and W.W.C.P. in forenoon. O.C. No.42 M.A.C. called in afternoon.	
	2/9/18.		Went with Q.M.S. to R.Q. Light Railways at ARTILLERY CORNER, ANZIN, to arrange for ambulance trucks to run from L'ABBAYETTE to ST.CATHERINE. Afterwards proceeded to A.D.S. L'ABBAYETTE, and informed M.O.i/c. of the arrangements made. Visited O.P. at RAMPOUX and also R.A.P. near single arch bridge. On return journey picked up pilot and observer of crashed aeroplane. On arrival at M.D.S. I met A.D.M.S. 49th Division. Went with him to Field Ambulance at MAROEUIL and met A.D.M.S. 51st Sign. Div. there. D.D.M.S. XXII Corps visited M.D.S. this afternoon.	5mm M.B: 6.27.
	3/9/18.		A.D.M.S. called in morning and went to A.D.S. to inspect the train arrangements. Closed QUARRY POST and withdrew N.C.O. and men to M.D.S. W.W.C.P. lorries to run to A.D.S. Called at W.W.C.P. and informed O.i/c. of new arrangements. Q.M. proceeds on leave. Capt. Moore to act as temp. Q.Master. O.C. 42 M.A.C. called in evening.	5mm 5mm
	4/9/18.		Called on A.D.M.S. and D.A.D.O.S. in morning regarding clothing for gassed patients. In afternoon visited M.D.S.; train-load of gassed cases had just left.	5mm
	5/9/18.		Visited A.D.S. in morning. Large number of gassed cases coming in; these are being evacuated by train, car and lorry. Returned to M.D.S. by train in afternoon.	5mm
	6/9/18.		Called at C.Rest Station at ANZIN in forenoon. Interviewed Os. C. Nos.2 and 15 C.C.Ss. about type of case being sent to C.R.S. A.D.M.S. called in afternoon. Col. Hume, Consulting Physician, First Army also called. He suggested that Major Melvin should take post as Physiologist with First Army. Capt. Craig, M.O. reported for duty with unit.	5mm
	7/9/18.		D.D.M.S. XXII Corps called in morning, along with D.A.& Q.M.G. and discussed the question of advance or M.D.S. in event of enemy retreating. Snowed. Went to 152 Inf. Bde. H.Q. and -- spints etc. Visited A.D.S. and met them again there. Afterwards saw Bde. Major who suggested the caves at ROEUX as site for main Dressing Station. I afterwards visited the caves, but considered them unsuitable owing to their being too deep. Roagarak Lunched at A.D.S. and returned to M.D.S. in afternoon.	5mm

WAR DIARY of 1/2nd Highland Field Ambulance, R.A.M.C. T.F.

INTELLIGENCE SUMMARY

Army Form C. 2118.

Vol. 41 Page 2.

Place	Date	Hour	Summary of Events and Information	Remarks and references to Appendices
ST.CATHERINE.	7/9/18.		The A.D.M.S. called later and I accompanied him to see D.D.M.S. XXII Corps concerning the above.	mmg
	8/9/18.		Very wet day. Visited A.D.S. in morning and walked with Capt. Roy to R.A.P. 1/7th Gord. Highrs. (I.7.b.1.5.).	mmg
	9/9/18.		Heavy rain again. Visited A.D.S. in morning. Capt. Craig relieves Lieut. Lurier, U.S.M.C. at A.D.S. in afternoon I called at A.D.M.S. O.C. 42 M.A.C. called in evening. Returned 20 bearers to 1/3rd Highd. Field Ambulance. Received complaint re cars not proceeding to workshop regularly (This is unavoidable while the Division is in the line).	mmg
	10/9/18.		A.D.M.S. came to A.D.S. in the morning, to examine men prior to visit from Med. Inspector of Drafts on the following day. Lieut. Lurier posted to 1/7th Arg. & Suthd. Highrs. in relief of Capt. Baing who joins this unit for duty. Serjt-major T. Kerr reported for duty in place of Sjt.major Gosling evacuated sick. Major Wallace rejoins unit on return of D.A.D.M.S. from leave to U.K.	mmg
	11/9/18.		Med. Inspector of Drafts arrived in morning and spent the whole day examining men of the XXII Corps. A.DS.M.S. 51st and 49th Divisions were both present. Visited A.D.S. in afternoon with Serjt-Major. Warned M.O.1/C. about approaching relief. Reported to A.D.M.S. in evening about orders for relief. Capt. Moore A.A.M.C. evacuated sick.to C.C.S. Advance party proceeded to GOUY SERVINS in afternoon to deal with sick of 152 Inf. Bde.	mmg
	12/9/18.		Along with Col. Rutherford, O.C. 1/3rd W.R. Field Ambulance, I visited A.D.S. and Car Collecting Post at FAMPOUX, SANDPITS and SINGLE ARCH BRIDGE. Returned via POINT DU JOUR to M.D.S. Made mutual arrangements about relief to be completed tomorrow. Advance party arrives for Main and Adv. Dressing Stations. Capt. Roy on relief returns from Adv. to Main Dressing Station. Reported to A.D.M.S. in evening on progress of relief. Major Melvin receives orders to proceed to 33 C.C.S. for duty. Lieut. Prather, M.O.R.C., U.S.A., reported for duty from 33 C.C.S.	mmg
	13/9/18.		Unit moved at 10 a.m. after handing over to O.C. 1/3rd W.R. Field Ambulance, via MONT ST. ELOI and VILLERS-au-BOIS, arriving at GOUY SERVINS at 1-45 p.m., and occupied the billets vacated by the 1/2nd W.R. Field Ambulance there. Major Melvin/	mmg

WAR DIARY of 1/2nd Highland Field Ambulance,
R.A.M.C. T.F.

INTELLIGENCE SUMMARY

(Erase heading not required.)

Army Form C. 2118.

Vol. 41. Page 3.

Place	Date	Hour	Summary of Events and Information	Remarks and references to Appendices
Our SERVICES.	13/9/18.		Major Melvin proceeded to 33 C.C.S. for duty. Called on A.D.M.S. in evening regarding vacant Majority. Make suggestion regarding the supply by each Field Ambulance in turn of Motor bicycle and Ford Ambulance car attached to A.D.M.S for duty.	nil
	14/9/18.		Detailed various working parties for duty with Town Major, R.Es., etc. Kit Inspection in morning. Capt. Craig, M.C., detailed for duty with 1/6th R.Highrs. in relief of Lieut. Philip admitted Hospital sick. Q.M. returns from leave.	nil
	15/9/18.		Brig.Gen. Segrave called in morning. A.D.M.S. called in afternoon regarding equipment of emergency Limber Wagon, extra stretchers etc.	nil
	16/9/18.		Held conference with Os.C. 1/3rd and 2/1st High. Field Amboes. at H.Q. 1/3rd H.F.A., ESTREE-CAUCHE, to arrange uniform scheme to return surplus equipment to Ordnance, (2) Loading of emergency limber wagon and (3) medical equipment of ambulance cars.	nil
	17/9/18.		Continued intensive training. Visited A.D.M.S. at MAROEUIL in afternoon. Internal economy being carried on.	nil
	18/9/18.		Opened ward for 20 patients in loft of Chateau. D.A.D.M.S. XXII Corps called. Tried experimental load on limber wagon and made out list of contents. Capt. Roy detailed to report to 2 C.C.S. (XXII Corps Rest Station). Capt. Gorrie, H.J. reported for duty from 1/3rd H.F.A. and taken on strength of unit.	nil
	19/9/18.		Called on A.D.M.S. in morning.	nil
	20/9/18.		Warning Order for Division to move received.	nil
	21/9/18.		Cleaning up transport vehicles for inspection by I.O.M. Called on A.D.M.S. on evening and got orders to move on 23rd. Bde. Movement order also received. Inspection of transport by I.O.M. did not take place. 22/9/18.	nil

WAR DIARY of 1/2nd Highland Field Ambulance, R.A.M.C. T.F. 2113.

Vol. 41. page 4.

INTELLIGENCE SUMMARY

(Erase heading not required.)

Place	Date	Hour	Summary of Events and Information	Remarks and references to Appendices
GOUY-SERVINS.	22/9/18.		Went to Maroeuil in morning. Called on A.D.M.S. and afterwards went to 1/2nd West Rid. F.A. to arrange about taking over. Capt. Gorrie with Advanced Party proceeded to Maroeuil in afternoon. Patients were sent on in evening.	
	23/9/18.		Unit moved to Maroeuil leaving Gouy at 10.30 a.m. via Villers au Bois and arrived at Maroeuil at 1.45 p.m.	
	24/9/18.		Lieut. Prather detailed for duty to 1/6th Seaforth Highlanders. Capt. Laing along with Ford Car proceeded in morning to 1/3rd High. Field Ambce. for temporary duty. A.D.M.S. called in forenoon.	
	25/9/18.		Called on O's.C., 1/3rd and 2/1st High. Field Ambces, regarding transfer of cases for Corps Rest Station. Held conference in afternoon to make final arrangements for load of wagon. (List of load attached). This wagon is a reserve of medical comforts, blankets, and splints, to be sent forward along with the limber wagons of the other two units in case of a rapid advance. Captain Roy rejoined unit from Corps Rest Station.	
	26/9/18.		Personnel employed cleaning up billets, etc. Fire Drill in afternoon. Captain Roy detailed to 1/3rd Highland Field Ambulance for temporary duty.	
	28/9/18.		Captain Roy rejoined from 1/3rd Highland Field Ambulance. Corps Rest Station now closed. Captain T.M. Metcalf reported for duty and taken on strength of unit.	
	29/9/18.		A.D.M.S. 51st Division and D.D.M.S. XXII Corps called in afternoon about dental arrangements.	
	30/9/18.		Hospital very full of patients. Arranged to pitch tents. Very stormy day.	

Army Form C. 2118.

WAR DIARY of 1/2nd Highland Field Ambce., R.A.M.C. T.F.

INTELLIGENCE SUMMARY

(Erase heading not required.) Vol.41 Page 5.

Instructions regarding War Diaries and Intelligence Summaries are contained in F. S. Regs., Part II. and the Staff Manual respectively. Title pages will be prepared in manuscript.

Place	Date	Hour	Summary of Events and Information	Remarks and references to Appendices
MAROIUIL.	30/9/18.		Capt. Gorrie, H.J. given authority to wear the badges of Major while commanding a Section of a Field Ambulance (51st High. Div. 36/160/A. 22/9/18).	nil
			George W. Miller Lieut. Col., O.C. 1/2nd Highland Field Ambulance, R.A.M.C. T.F.	

Contents of Emergency Limber Wagon.

Contents of front Half.

Blankets, G.S.	40.
Gooch splinting, rolls	2.
Sandbags	25.
Back leg splints, padded	6.
Rectangular arm splints	6.
Shell Dressings	200.
Cotton Wool lbs	15.
Gauze, rolls	48.
Bandages, flannel	36.
" 6"	36.
" 4"	100.
" 3"	100.
" 2"	50.
" triangular	36.
Tow lbs	10.
Plaster, adhesive, 2"	6.
" 4"	3.
Depage Humerus splints	6.
Eupad lbs	1.
Sol. Acid Picric 1% Ozs	48.
" 50% "	2.
Basins, Washing 11"	1.
Nail Brush, Soap	1.
Towels, hand, hospital	2.
Scissors, prs 2. SafetyPins Boxes 2.
Stomach Warmer 1. Forceps, Pressure 2.
A.B. 152, 153, 153b, 166. O.C. 1/2nd Highland Field Ambulance, R.A.M.C. T.F.

Contents of rear half.

Soyer's stove, complete	1.
Cooks' Ladles	1.
Thomas' Splints	6.
Suspension bars	6.
Pannikins, pint	20.
Enamel jugs, large	1.
Blankets, G.S.	10.
Tea lbs	6.
Sugar "	22.
Milk tins	48.
Biscuits, fancy, "	8.
Coal Cwts	½
Wood qty.	
Dixies	1.
Lamps, hurricane	2.
Cans, oil 9½ pts.	1.
Axe, felling	1.
Pickaxe	1.
Shovel, G.S.	1.
Feeders, enamel	1.
Candles	24.

signature

Lieut-Col.,

30/9/18.

1/2nd Highland F.A.

Army Form C. 2118

WAR DIARY of 1/2nd Highland Field Ambulance, R.A.M.C. T.F.

INTELLIGENCE SUMMARY. Vol. 42 page 1.

(Erase heading not required.)

Instructions regarding War Diaries and Intelligence Summaries are contained in F. S. Regs., Part II. and the Staff Manual respectively. Title pages will be prepared in manuscript.

Place	Date	Hour	Summary of Events and Information	Remarks and references to Appendices
MAROEUIL.	1/10/18.		Warning Order received for Divisional move. 1/2nd remains at MAROEUIL. Capt. Laing rejoins unit from 1/3rd H.F.A.	nil
	2/10/18.		Called on O.C. 2/1st H.F.A. at ECOIVRES in morning regarding men returning from hospital deficient of kit. These are all gassed cases. Capt. Metcalfe rejoins unit from 1/3rd H.F.A. 21 O.R. rejoin from 1/3rd H.F.A.	nil
	3/10/18.		A.D.M.S. called.	nil
	4/10/18.		New Bath house nearly completed.	nil
	5/10/18.		Called on A.D.M.S. at CHATEAU d'ACQ, and met O.C. 2/1st H.F.A. there. A.D.M.S. called in afternoon. Orders received for Divisional move to BOURLON WOOD sector.	nil
	6/10/18.		Called at H.Q. 153rd Inf. Bde. with regard to move. D.D.M.S. Canadian Corps. called to inspect ambulance site. Concert for men in evening. Very successful. Orders received postponing move for 24 hours. These were cancelled later.	nil
	7/10/18.		Called at H.Q. 153rd Inf. Bde. and received orders regarding move. Proceeded in afternoon along with Major Mallace to INCHY to arrange about taking over from Canadian Field Ambulance. Dined with Serjeants in evening. Orders for embussing received at night. Destination changed.	nil
	8/10/18.		Called at H.Q. 153rd Inf. Bde. in morning regarding destination. Site at INCHY impracticable 153rd Inf. Bde alloted site at QUEANT. Informed by D.A.D.M.S. 4th Can. Division that the 13th Canadian Field Ambulance will take over hospital site occupied by this unit today. Proceeded in car with Major Mallace to QUEANT. Met Staff Captain 153rd Inf. Bde. and secured site. Transport under Lieut. & Q.M. Johnston marched at 06-30 arrived at QUEANT at 14-00 hours. Called at H.Q.	nil

WAR DIARY of 1/2nd Highland Field Ambulance, Army Form C. 2118.

or

INTELLIGENCE SUMMARY. R.A.M.C. T.F.

(Erase heading not required.) Vol.42 Page 2.

Instructions regarding War Diaries and Intelligence
Summaries are contained in F. S. Regs., Part II.
and the Staff Manual respectively. Title pages
will be prepared in manuscript.

Place	Date	Hour	Summary of Events and Information	Remarks and references to Appendices
	8/10/18	continued.	Called at H.Q. 153rd Inf. Bde. in afternoon and asked for trench covers to make bivouacs. I received 13 from Major Paulin, Cmg. Can. Field Ambce. Tents pitched and bivouacs erected in evening preparatory to unit arriving. Unit under Major Gorrie embussed at ECURIE at 08-00 en route for QUEANT. 4 bearers detailed to each of the 3 Btns. of 153rd Inf. Bde.	inits
	9/10/18.		Unit arrived at QUEANT at 02-00. Vicinity shelled in morning by H.V. fragments flying through the camp. Moved camp to safer site. A.D.M.S. called in afternoon. Capt. Metcalfe proceeded to take temporary Méd. Charge of 51st D.A.C. in relief of Capt. Grant.	inits
Starting Point PRONVILLE	10/10/18.		Orders received during night to march at 14-47. Struck camp in forenoon and packed up. Marched at 14-00 via PRONVILLE, MOEUVRES, and ANNEUX CHAPELLE, to BOURLON, Long march over bad road. Inspected en route by Major General Carter Campbell, G.O.C. Division and Bgdr. Gen. Green, 153rd Inf. Bde. Arrived BOURLON Village at 19-00. Lieut. Johnston and transport arrived at 21-00.	inits
	11/10/18.		Orders received at 05-00 to be prepared to move at 10-00. Loaded up and stood by. Arranged with AD.M.S. to hand over surplus Medical Stores to O.C. 1/3rd High. F.Ambce. At 13-00 orders were received to move at 15-00. 12th Field Ambulance take over. Do not move off till 17 hours. Very slow delayed march. Roads badly blocked with traffic owing to lack of traffic control. After repeated delays, decided to march in single file along the side of road. Messenger delivers verbal message to proceed to TILLOY, but as billets have already been prepared at MORENCHIES I proceed there as previously arranged, arriving at 23-30. Transport arrive 30 mins later. Orders received from A.D.M.S. to move to ESCAUDOEUVRES in morning, the unit to be detached from 153rd Inf. Bde.	inits
	12/10/18.		Marched at 07-00 to ESCAUDOEUVRES. Billeted in CONVENT along with 2/1st H.F.A. Take over Main Dressing Station at 18-00. 1/3rd H.F.A. arrived at 18-00. Casualties fairly numerous. No busses available for Walking Wounded. Capt. Laing and 16 bearers detailed for duty with 2/1st H.F.A.	inits
	13/10/18.		300 Walking cases in Dressing Station and no busses for evacuation of same. Busses/.	inits

WAR DIARY of 1/2nd Highland Field Ambulance, Army Form C. 2118.
R.A.M.C. T.F.

INTELLIGENCE SUMMARY. Vol. 42 page 3.

Place	Date	Hour	Summary of Events and Information	Remarks and references to Appendices
ESCAUDOEUVRES.	13/10/18.		Busses arrived about 11-00. A.D.M.S. called in forenoon and again in afternoon. 17 O.R. detailed for duty with 2/1st High. F. Ambulance. All available men employed screening windows, removing filth and improvising heating etc. A.Ds. M.S. 4th and 49th Divisions called. Large number of casualties being admitted. Dressing Station full of stretcher and walking cases. O.C. 1/3rd West Riding F.A. called regarding a similar congestion of cases at his Dressing Station. Arranged to accommodate about 200 of his walking cases if necessary. Rearranged Dressing and Reception Rooms. In evening 200 walking cases and 70 Stretcher cases awaiting evacuation.	nil
	14/10/18.		All walking cases cleared by busses during night. 40 stretcher cases remained in morning. Quiet morning. A.D.M.S. called. Went with O.C. 42 M.A.C. to locate railhead of Light railway. Found same at MORENCHIES. D.D.M.S. XXII Corps called in forenoon, regarding change of arrangements. This unit now deals with stretcher cases of 49th and 51st Divisions. 49th Division similarly deals with walking cases. Capt. Squair, R.A.M.C. and Capt. Williams, U.S.M.C. report for duty. Buildings now greatly improved, a large amount of work having been done on same. A.T.S. given and Official Records Kept as from 17-00 this date.	nil
	15/10/18.		Continue cleaning up buildings. A.D.M.S. called in morning and very much impressed with the work which had been accomplished. Accompanied A.D.M.S. to A.D.S. to reconnoitre in view of a possible move forward. D.M.S. First Army and D.D.M.S. XXII Corps called during my absence. Capt Williams, U.S.M.C. proceeds to 1/5th Sea. Highrs. to replace M.O. of that Batn. who has been gassed.	nil
	16/10/18.		Quiet day. A.D.M.S. called in forenoon, and G.O.C. Division in afternoon. Capt. Squair detailed for duty as M.O. i/c. Reception Camp at ECOIVRES.	nil
	17/10/18.		Still quiet. Went with A.Ds. M.S. 49th and 51st Divisions to CAMBRAI to be shewn site for Corps Rest Station. Lieut-Col. Bruce attached for instruction.	nil
	18/10/18.		A.D.M.S. called in morning, leaving orders to hand over to 1/3rd H.F.A. and proceed to CAMBRAI in afternoon to prepare a wing of building for Div. Rest Station. Went/	nil

WAR DIARY of 1/2nd Highland Field Ambulance, R.A.M.C. T.F.

INTELLIGENCE SUMMARY

Army Form C. 2118.

Vol. 42 page 4.

Instructions regarding War Diaries and Intelligence Summaries are contained in F. S. Regs., Part II. and the Staff Manual respectively. Title pages will be prepared in manuscript.

Place	Date	Hour	Summary of Events and Information	Remarks and references to Appendices
	18/10/18.		Went with Quartermaster and Sjt.Major in forenoon to inspect building. Sent advance party at 14-00 under charge of Major Gorrie. Main body followed at 15-30. Area Commandant called at 17-00 and said that as no ambulances are allowed in CAMBRAI, unit must move in morning. Along with Major GOOD, 49th Div. I went to NAVES and reported to A.Ds.M.S. 49th and 51st Divisions. I then reported to DD.M.S. XXII Corps, thereafter returning to CAMBRAI.	inig
	19/10/18.		20 O.R. detailed for duty with 35th F. Amb. at HOPITAL NORMALE, CAMBRAI. Received orders to move unit back to ESCAUDOEUVRES. A.D.M.S. called in forenoon. March at 13-30 and take over billets evacuated by 1/3rd H.F.A. in CONVENT, ESCAUDOEUVRES. Received orders to meet A.D.M.S. at THUN ST. MARTIN at 8-00. tomorrow. Unit to be ready to move at the same hour.	inig
	20/10/18.		Met the A.D.M.S. at THUN ST. MARTIN and proceeded with him to A.D.S. IWUY. Ordered to move to IWUY as soon as possible. On return called on D.D.M.S. XXII Corps. regarding move. Unit marching party had chosen site for Main Dressing Station at CHATEAU d'IWUY, at present occupied by 4th Can. Inf. Bde. Who are moving out. Prepare Dressing Room and open as Main Dressing Station at 17-00. A.D.M.S. called at 16-00. Casualties few. M.A.C. cars arrived at 19-00.	inig
	21/10/18.		All spare men employed cleaning up CHATEAU and surroundings. German booby trap exploded in incinerator. (Bomb hidden in dirty mattress.). One corporal seriously wounded and one man slightly. A.D.M.S. called in forenoon along with O.C. 2/1st H.F.A. D.D.M.S. called in afternoon. Called on A.D.M.S. in evening.	inig
	22/10/18.		Can. Bde. left CHATEAU at 10-30. A.D.M.S. called in morning. Casualties still few. Personnel who were billetted in village now moved to CHATEAU grounds, transport occupying CHATEAU stables. Much cleaning still necessary.	inig
	23/10/18.		Cleaning continued. A.D.M.S. called in afternoon, instructing me to proceed to PAVE DE VALENCIENNES to look out for Main Dressing Station there. Procured fairly good position in Factory there, the only disadvantage being the long narrow road approaching same. Reported result to A.D.M.S. at AVESNES LE SEC, and arranged to move in morning. Major Gorrie with Adv. party proceeded tonight to hold new site, and prepare same. Col. Bruce/	inig

WAR DIARY of 1/2nd Highland Field Ambulance, R.A.M.C. T.F.

INTELLIGENCE SUMMARY.

Vol. 42, Page 5.

Place	Date	Hour	Summary of Events and Information	Remarks and references to Appendices
ENCIENNES	24/10/18.		Col. Bruce goes on to join Major Gorrie. Unit marches at 08-00. arriving at PAVE DE VAL-ENCIENNES at 09-00. Main Dressing Station there already open and working. 150 wounded arrived up to 18-00. Great difficulties experienced in heating place. This improves as the day goes on. A.D.M.S. 51st Div. called along with D.D.M.S.. XXII Corps. In afternoon I proceeded to DOUCHY to inspect A.D.S. with a view to Main Dress. Station moving forward. On return I reported at H.Q. Extra stretchers and blankets arrive from Corps Dump.	init
	25/10/18.		Very quiet morning. A.D.M.S. called at 13-00. At this time cases begin to arrive and continue all day. Went with Serjt.Major in afternoon to DOUCHY to procure site for Main Dressing Station. Secure good site at ECOLE DES FILLES, HASPRES ROAD. Arranged with Town Major to clear building tomorrow morning. Reported suggested arrangements to A.D.M.S. On return to Main Dressing Station I arranged for Adv. party to proceed in morning to DOUCHY.	init
	26/10/18.		I accompanied advance party to DOUCHY at 08-00. Large amount of cleaning to be done. Three feet of old manure had to be removed from tiled floor of schoolroom. Other rooms were in a similar state. A.D.M.S. called in forenoon. Dressing Station ready for receiving patients at 13-00. Main Dressing Station at PAVE DE VALENCIENNES closed at 14-00 and unit moved forward to DOUCHY, arriving at 14-30. A.D.S. moved to PYRAMIDE DE DEMAIN. Casualties arrive steadily all afternoon and evening. A.D.M.S. 11th Div. called.	init
	27/10/18.		Capt. Roy proceeded on leave to U.K. A.D.M.S. called in forenoon along with A.D.M.S. 49th Div. O.C. 1/2nd W. Rid. F.A. inspected Main Dressing Station preparatory to taking over. Large number of French civilians receive food and Medical treatment. Consulted with Os.C. 1/1st and 1/2nd W. Rid. F.Ambulances, and to facilitate move, send Major Gorrie, with all surplus men to NEUVILLE, to make room for 1/2nd W. RID. F.Ambce. which has to vacate old billets today, and which is taking over Main Dressing Station. A.D.M.S. and O.C. 2/1st H.F.A. called at midday. Went to NEUVILLE in afternoon and Major Gorrie and party arrived while I was there. On return to Main Dressing Station I found that 1/2nd W. Rid. F.A. had arrived.	init
	29/10/18.		Marched at 9-00 to NEUVILLE and took over billets vacated by 1/1st W. Rid. F.A. Unloaded all wagons and rearranged equipment. Returned surplus dressings and splints to M.D.S. Capt. Metcalfe rejoined from 51st D.A.C. and Capt. Laing from 2/1st H.F.A.	init

Capt. Metcalfe/

Army Form C. 2118.

WAR DIARY of 1/2nd High. Field Ambulance, R.A.M.C. T.F.

INTELLIGENCE SUMMARY.   Vol. 42, page 6.

(Erase heading not required.)

Instructions regarding War Diaries and Intelligence Summaries are contained in F. S. Regs., Part II. and the Staff Manual respectively. Title pages will be prepared in manuscript.

Place	Date	Hour	Summary of Events and Information	Remarks and references to Appendices
	30/10/18.		Capt. Metcalfe proceeded for duty with 256 Bde. R.F.A. Three officers spent all forenoon visiting civilian sick. Over 150 visits. A.D.M.S. called in forenoon and informed me that 152 Inf. Bde. Group is moving today, and as no orders have been received I proceed to Bde. H.Q. at DOUCHY, and find that Bde. has not been informed that this unit has rejoined that Group. Bde. moved to THUN ST. MARTIN area, and I arranged to send billeting party tonight to secure billets. Capt. Laing with Tent Subdivision are sent to 22 C.C.S. CAMBRAI for duty there.	initl.
	31/10/18.		Unit moves at 09-00 via IWUY to THUN ST. MARTIN arriving there at 11-30. Spent day in cleaning-up billets and surroundings. 36 gassed cases admitted from 1/6th Sea. Highrs. and were detained overnight as Div. and Corps Rest Stations were both full. Total of Casualties in personnel during operations......Gassed....6 O.R.	initl.
	1/11/18.			

O.C. 1/2nd Highland Field Ambulance, R.A.M.C. T.F.

George W. Miller
Lieut-Col.,

SUMMARY OF CASUALTIES.

	Officers.	O.R.
ESCAUDOEUVRES.....{Unofficially recorded............ (16-00 14/10/18 to 14-00 18th.) Officially recorded...........	29 10	832. 273.
IWUY..	4	62.
PAVE DE VALENCIENNES................................	22	314.
DOUCHY..	16	144.
TOTALS.	81	1625.

160/3401

1/2- M.H.T.O.

COMMITTEE FOR THE
MEDICAL HISTORY OF THE WAR.
Date 16 JAN 1919

16/1/18

WAR DIARY OF 1/2nd Highland Field Ambulance, R.A.M.C., T.F.

INTELLIGENCE SUMMARY.

Vol. 43. Page 1.

(Erase heading not required.)

Army Form C. 2118.

Place	Date	Hour	Summary of Events and Information	Remarks and references to Appendices
THUN-ST-MARTIN.	1-11-18.		Personnel engaged cleaning up village, road repairing etc. Visited M.G.Bn. to arrange about Medical attendance. Captain Squair detailed to proceed from Reception Camp to M.G.Bn.	
	2-11-18.		D.A.D.M.S. called in morning. I called at Brigade H. Qrs. in forenoon re hospital accomodation and was alloted a billet for the purpose.	
	3-11-18.		Major Gorrie relieved Captain Laing at No. 22 C.C.S. Called on Battalion M.Os and inspected Sanitary arrangements. Arranged to work small Bath-house in Thun-ST-Martin.	
	4-11-18.		Staff Captain 152 Brigade called in forenoon. Bath-house almost ready for use. Captain Laing proceeds on leave.	
	5-11-18.		Heavy rain all day.	
	6-11-18.		Still raining. Called on A.D.M.S. in forenoon. Major Mallace goes to DOUCHY to arrange attendance on sick civilians. Captain Hewitt reported for duty. Orders re Ceremonial parade to be held in VALENCIENNES received. Major Mallace with Lieut.Col.Bruce and Tent Subdivision proceed to DOUCHY to attend civilian sick.	
	7-11-18.		A.D.M.S. Lieut. Johnston with party proceed to VALENCIENNES to attend Ceremonial parade. Called in morning. Went to DOUCHY in afternoon to see how arrangements were going.	
	8-11-18.		Went with A.D.M.S. to NEUVILLE and interviewed Maire of that village. A large number of sick requiring attention there. Captain Cathcart 2/1st Highland Field Ambulance detailed with sufficient personnel and equipment of 1/3rd Highland Field Ambulance to open Dispensary at NEUVILLE. Large quantities of Bones, Medical Comforts etc., sent to these villages.	
	9-11-18.		Medical attendance on civilians extended to FAMARS and HAULCHIN. Order from A.D.M.S. to detail Captain Hewitt with personnel and equipment for these villages. Q.M.S. goes to ARRAS with lorry for Medical Comforts, etc. An extra Car detailed for duty at DOUCHY.	

Army Form C. 2118.

WAR DIARY OF 1/2nd Highland Field Ambulance, R.A.M.C., T.F.

INTELLIGENCE SUMMARY.

(Erase heading not required.) Vol. 43. Page 2.

Place	Date	Hour	Summary of Events and Information	Remarks and references to Appendices
THUN-ST-MARTIN.	10-11-18.		Called at Brigade H.Qrs. in morning re Bath-house arrangements.	A.44
	11-11-18.		General holiday throughout the Division owing to ARMISTICE being signed. Torch light procession and Bon-Fire in evening.	A.44
	12-11-18.		Order by A.D.M.S. to represent R.A.M.C. on Divisional Sports Committee. Meeting with O.C. 1/8th Royal Scots, ESTRUN at 14-00hours, afterwards went with Sgt. Lawson to 1/3rd Highland Field Ambulance thence with Major Hunter and his Committee to 2/1st H.F.AmB., where meeting was held to draw up details.	A.44
	13-11-18.		Beaumont-Hamel dinner in evening. Secured Hall in R.E. Dump close to village. Men on duty at DOUCHY and No. 22 C.C.S. allowed to attend as far as possible. A.D.M.S. also attends dinner.	
	14-11-18.		Papers regarding alleged looting of wine at BUSNES CHATEAU received. G.O.C. Division called in afternoon and addressed the men. Captain Roy rejoined from leave. Called on A.D.M.S. in evening re alleged looting at BUSNES CHATEAU. Requested Division to hold Court of Enquiry to get it thoroughly cleared up.	
	15-11-18.		Called on A.D.M.S. in morning regarding transport of blankets and wheeled stretcher carriers. Major Gorrie with party returned from No. 22 C.C.S.	
	16-11-18.		Called at NEUVILLE and DOUCHY in forenoon visiting A.D.M.S. en route. Transport vehicles inspected by I.O.M. Captain Squair reports for duty.	
	17-11-18.		Went to ESTRUN in morning to look for billets and was offered billets of 1/8th Royal Scots who are expected to move. Captain Roy ordered to report to D.D.M.S. XXII Corps for duty as D.A.D.M.S.	
	18-11-18.		Sent advanced party to ESTRUN to hold billets. Interview with M.O. 1/6th Sea. Highrs. regarding disposal of cases.	
	19-11-18.		Court of Enquiry held in forenoon. Evidence of witnesses available heard and enquiry adjourned pending return from leave of other witnesses.	

WAR DIARY OF 1/2nd Highland Field Ambulance, R.A.M.C., (T.F.)

INTELLIGENCE SUMMARY.

Army Form C. 2118.

Vol. 43. Page 3.

(Erase heading not required.)

Instructions regarding War Diaries and Intelligence Summaries are contained in F. S. Regs., Part II. and the Staff Manual respectively. Title pages will be prepared in manuscript.

Place	Date	Hour	Summary of Events and Information	Remarks and references to Appendices
THUN-ST-MARTIN.	19-11-18.		Advanced party recalled from ESTRUN as move of 1/8th Royal Scots is cancelled.	
	20-11-18.		Went to ESTRUN to look for other billets but found none satisfactory. Secured good site in IWUY and arranged to move tomorrow. Lecture on Wireless Telegraphy in afternoon.	
IWUY.	21-11-18.		Working party and part of transport moved to IWUY in forenoon. Billets in THUN-ST-MARTIN handed over to 1/6th Sea. Highrs. and remainder of Unit move in afternoon. Captain Squair relieved Major Mallace at DOUCHY.	
	22-11-18.		Visited sick civilians in IWUY in forenoon. Visited NEUVILLE and DOUCHY in afternoon.	
	23-11-18.		Visited sick civilians in IWUY.	
	24-11-18.		Visited sick civilians. Church parade at 10-45 hours in Cinema at IWUY. Captain Laing rejoined from leave.	
	25-11-18.		Lieut. Colonel Miller proceeds on leave. Major A.C.Mallace assumes Command. Visited civilian sick. Early treatment room established at Hospital for treatment of venereal contacts.	
	26-11-18.		Visited civilian sick. Lecture to personnel on prophylactic measures against venereal disease. By order of A.D.M.S. 51st (Highland) Division Major H.J.Gorrie instructed to report to O.C. 1/3rd Highland Field Ambulance for Duty and struck off strength of this Unit this date.	
	27-11-18.		Visited sick civilians. Lieut. Colonel Bruce rejoined from DOUCHY.	
	28-11-18.		Visited sick civilians. Lecture by the Revd. W.P.Gillieson, Senior Chaplain, 51st (Highland) Division----Subject "FROM WAR TO WORK".	
	29-11-18.		Visited civilian sick. Advance party of One Officer and three Other ranks left for new area.	
	30-11-18.		Visited civilian sick.	

Army Form C. 2118.

WAR DIARY OF 1/2ND HIGHLAND FIELD AMBULANCE, R.A.M.C., (T.F.)

INTELLIGENCE SUMMARY.

Vol. 43. Page 4.

(Erase heading not required).

Instructions regarding War Diaries and Intelligence Summaries are contained in F. S. Regs., Part II. and the Staff Manual respectively. Title pages will be prepared in manuscript.

Place	Date	Hour	Summary of Events and Information	Remarks and references to Appendices
IWUY.	30-11-18.		Miniature Scottish National Flags issued by St. Andrew's Society and authorised to be worn on St. Andrew's Day. The Divisional Sports held to-day on ground North of THUN L'EVEQUE. Report rendered to A.D.M.S. on Sanitary Condition of the Brigade Area.	

J E Maguire

Major,
A/O. C. 1/2nd Highland Field Ambulance, R.A.M.C.(T).

1/2nd Highland F.A.

COMMITTEE FOR THE
MEDICAL HISTORY OF THE WAR
Date 6 MAR. 1919

Army Form C. 2118.

WAR DIARY
or
INTELLIGENCE SUMMARY.

1/2nd Highland Field Ambulance, R.A.M.C., T.F.   Vol. 44 page 1.

(Erase heading not required.)

Place	Date	Hour	Summary of Events and Information	Remarks and references to Appendices
IWUY.	1-12-18.		Church parade in Cinema, IWUY. Extension of Service, as per G.R.O. No. 5691, communicated to all ranks.	
	2-12-18.		Captain Squair and detached party on duty at DOUCHY rejoined unit today. Letters of thanks received from Maire and population of FAMARS for work done by Officers and men of this unit for the Civilian sick.	
	3-12-18.		No. 56157 Pte. W. Boyd, M.M., awarded the Medaille Militaire for gallantry in the field.	
	4-12-18.		G.O.C., 51st Highland Division, inspected hospital in forenoon.	
	5-12-18.		Orders received from A.D.M.S. for Lieut. Colonel Bruce to take over Command of the 1/3rd Highland Field Ambulance in place of Lieut. Colonel Foggie, D.S.O.	
	6-12-18.		Captain Craig reported for duty from 1/6th Royal Highlanders and taken on strength of this unit as from 1st December 1918. A.D.M.S. called in forenoon. Visited Brigade Headquarters. Weekly sanitary report rendered.	
	7-12-18.		About 80 refugees, mostly women and children, who were "en passage", were fed by the unit.	
	8-12-18.		Visited A.D.M.S. today.	
	9-12-18.		Lecture by Captain Christie on "Burns the Man and Poet" at 14-30 hours in Recreation Room. Dancing Class instituted as part of Recreational Training.	
	10-12-18.		Captain Squair made inventory of Corps Dump at HASPRES on behalf of D.D.M.S., XXII Corps. First demobilisation orders received for three miners of unit.	
	11-12-18.		A lecture entitled "Drama" delivered by Lieut. Adams at 14-30 hours.	
	12-12-18.		A lecture entitled " Care of Disabled Soldiers" delivered by Captain Squair in lecture room at 14-00 hours.	

Army Form C. 2118.

WAR DIARY
for 1/2nd Highland Field Ambulance,
INTELLIGENCE SUMMARY. R.A.M.C., T.F.

Vol. 44 page 2.

(Erase heading not required.)

Instructions regarding War Diaries and Intelligence Summaries are contained in F. S. Regs., Part II. and the Staff Manual respectively. Title pages will be prepared in manuscript.

Place	Date	Hour	Summary of Events and Information	Remarks and references to Appendices
IWUY.	13-12-18.		Unit moved to BOIS DU LUC by motor lorries;today, via VALENCIENNES and MONS for preparation of Rest Station there in view of Division moving to that area at a later date. Lorries left IWUY at 08-00 hours and arrived BOIS du LUC at 15-00 hours. Horse Transport followed by easy stages.	
	14-12-18.		Took over Civil Hospital at BOIS du LUC and made the necessary arrangements for the reception of sick. Lieut. Colonel Miller returned from leave.	
	15-12-18.		Transport arrived in afternoon. Received warning that D.D.M.S. XXII Corps was to bring several Norwegian Officers to visit Ambulance. Made the necessary arrangements for inspection by them.	
	16-12-18.		Inspection cancelled. Arranged with Manager of Mines for erection of Cookhouse, Latrines, etc.	
	17-12-18.		Sent to British Red Cross for Stores.	
	18-12-18.		D.D.M.S. XXII Corps called and inspected Hospital. A.D.M.S. 51st (Highland) Division proceeded on leave to United Kingdom. Lieut. Johnston proceeded on leave to United Kingdom.	
	19-12-18.		Major Mallace proceeded on leave to United Kingdom. Drew 90 Iron beds and timber for Pack Store from Hospice at La Louviere. Under Authority granted by His Majesty The King the Field Marshall Commanding-in-Chief awarded the following decorations for gallantry on the Field. MILITARY CROSS. Captain A. C. Laing. BAR TO DISTINGUISHED CONDUCT MEDAL. No. M2/053918 Pte. A. E. Highmore, D.C.M., M.M.	
	20-12-18.		Went to Divisional Headquarters at IWUY and consulted with A/A.D.M.S. regarding various matters in connection with the Hospital.	
	21-12-18.		Returned to BOIS-DU-LUC from IWUY. Lieut. & Q.M. Johnston promoted to rank of Captain (Authority W.O. 183690/1 dated 18-12-18).	

Army Form C. 2118.

WAR DIARY OF 1/2nd Highland Field Ambulance, R.A.M.C.(T).
INTELLIGENCE SUMMARY.

(Erase heading not required.) vol. 44. Page 3.

Place	Date	Hour	Summary of Events and Information	Remarks and references to Appendices
BOIS-DU-LUC	24-12-18.		Went to IWUY to arrange about disinfection of blankets and collection of Stores, etc. Returned to Headquarters same day.	
	25-12-18.		Holiday. Christmas Dinner for men at 13 hours with concert in afternoon. Authority granted by G.O.C. 51st (Highland) Division for Captain D.D.CRAIG to wear the badges of Major whilst commanding a section of 1/2nd Highland Field Ambulance.(Authy. H.D.No.36/214A dated 22-12-18).	
	26-12-18.		Called on D.D.M.S. XXII Corps regarding construction of Disinfestor and Scabies Bath House, also saw C.R.E. about same. Dance was held in evening for personnel.	
	28-12-18.		Went to Mons in morning. Left indent for material for Bath House with D.D.M.S.	
	29-12-18.		Visited 1/3rd Highland Field Ambulance Site at SENEFFE along with Lieut. Colonel Bruce.	
	30-12-18.		Colonel McDougall, A.D.M.S. 52nd Division A/D.D.M.S. XXII Corps visited Hospital in forenoon. Arranged with Manager of Mines to provide horses for haulage of timber.	
	31-12-18.		Divisional Holiday. Concert and Dance in evening. Re Educational Work during December 1918. During the month Elementary Education classes have been held in Arithmetic, English, French, Geography, History and Civics. L/Cpl. Thomson and Pte. Wattison have been instructors and both have carried on the work with fidelity and zeal. One hour in the forenoon and one in the afternoon have been set apart for instruction. Great enthusiasm is being displayed by a number of the men who have realised the importance of preparing for, refreshing themselves for their future civil life, but as the Ambulance has been engaged in active duties some difficulty has been experienced in making satisfactory arrangements. In addition to the classes, Lectures have been delivered on popular and instructive subjects, e.g., Robbie Burns, The Drama, Prevention and treatment of Venereal Disease in civil life, Field Ambulance Experiences in the East, etc. On the whole the work has progressed favourably and is being supplemented by voluntary classes, viz., Chemistry and French conversation.	

George W. Mills
LIEUT. COL. R.A.M.C.
O.C. 1/2nd HIGHLAND FIELD AMB.

140/3490

51 DIV
Box 2706

1/2nd Highland F. A.

Journal

Army Form C. 2118.

WAR DIARY
or
INTELLIGENCE SUMMARY.
(Erase heading not required.)

1/2nd Highland Field Ambulance, R.A.M.C., T.F.

Vol. 45 page 1.

Place	Date	Hour	Summary of Events and Information	Remarks and references to Appendices
BOIS-DU-LUC.	6-1-19.		Extract from Supplement to London Gazette dated 30-12-18. T/4/241173 S.S.M. McKAY, J. mentioned in Sir Douglas Haig's despatch of 8-11-18.	
	7-1-19.		A Pamphlet entitled "Trade at Home" was read by Captain Squair in men's Mess Room.	
	8-1-19.		D.M.S. First Army visited Hospital in afternoon along with A/D.D.M.S. XXII Corps.	
	9-1-19.		Major Craig, D. proceeded on leave to U.K. Captain Laing to act as Q.M., during his absence.	
	10-1-19.		A Lecture entitled "Solar System" was delivered by Private Casey. Took over duties as A/A.D.M.S. 51st (Highland) Division this date.	
	12-1-19.		A Concert to welcome 152 Brigade was given by Local Band, BOIS-DU-LUC. Brigadier-General Segrave attended same.	
	14-1-19.		A Lecture entitled "J.J.ROUSSEAU" was delivered by Pte. Stewart, C.M.	
	16-1-19.		The u/m have been awarded the CROIX de GUERRE. (Authority:- XXII CORPS No.A 2383/30 d/-11-1-19.) WITH GOLD STAR. Captain Laing, A.C. (M.C.) WITH SILVER STAR. Lieut. Col. George W. Miller, D.S.O. WITH BRONZE STAR. No. 305054 S.Sgt. Cameron, A. " " " M2/021058 A/QMS.Gregory, E. (M.M.) Captain H.W.Browne, M.C. reported for duty this date, and will act as Transport Officer.	
	20-1-19.		A.D.M.S. returned from leave. Serjt. Major Kerr, T. despatched for demobilization. Q.M.S. Brown to act as Serjt. Major temporarily. S.Sgt. Smith, A. L. to act as Q.M.S. temporarily.	
	21-1-19.		A.D.M.S. inspected Rest Station. I delivered lecture to personnel on "Demobilization difficulties".	
	22-1-19.		Captain F.W.Squair proceeded on leave to U.K. Captain Laing appointed Educational Officer during absence of Captain Squair. No. 303054 S/Serjt. Cameron, A., awarded M.S.M., (Authority Supplement to London Gazette dated 18-1-19.)	
	28-1-19.		Lieut. A.E. McGregor delivered a lecture entitled "Modern Journalism".	
	30-1-19.		A.D.M.S. called.	

Army Form C. 2118.

WAR DIARY
for 1/2nd Highland Field Ambulance, R.A.M.C., T.F.
INTELLIGENCE SUMMARY. Vol. 45 page 2.
(Erase heading not required.)

Instructions regarding War Diaries and Intelligence Summaries are contained in F.S. Regs., Part II. and the Staff Manual respectively. Title pages will be prepared in manuscript.

Place	Date	Hour	Summary of Events and Information	Remarks and references to Appendices
			NOTE.— Education went on during the month in spite of difficulties owing to demobilisation of teachers. Relations with inhabitants have been excellent throughout the month. Horses belonging to the unit have been lent to Charbonnage for haulage of timber from neighbouring woods in return for which much material and help of every kind has been given to the unit by Société, Charbonnage.	Sgd.

George W. Miller
LIEUT. COL., R.A.M.C., T.F.
O.C. 1/2nd HIGHLAND FIELD AMBULANCE

[Stamp: 1/2nd HIGHLAND FIELD AMBULANCE — 1 FEB 1919 — R.A.M.C. (T) B.E.F.]

2nd Highland Field Amb.

Army Form C. 2115.

WAR DIARY
or
INTELLIGENCE SUMMARY.

(Erase heading not required.)

Instructions regarding War Diaries and Intelligence Summaries are contained in F. S. Regs., Part II. and the Staff Manual respectively. Title pages will be prepared in manuscript.

Place	Date	Hour	Summary of Events and Information	Remarks and references to Appendices
Bois du Luc.	8/2/19.		Major Craig rejoined from Leave.	
	11/2/19.		A Lecture by Lieut.Keay of the 51stH.G.O.,subject "Political Economy".	
	14/2/19.		Lieut.Colonel Miller proceeds on Leave, and Major Craig takes command during his absence. Q.M's Store broken into during the night. Visited A.P.M. in connection with burglary.	
	17/2/19.		Court of Enquiry held re Articles stolen from Q.M's Store.	
	19/2/19.		Colonel Gray, Skin Specialist inspected the Hospital and exressed his appreciation of the arrangements.	
	21/2/19.		Recommendation for Staff Sgt.Smith to be appointed Sgt.Major, approved.	
	22/2/19.		D.D.M.S. called in forenoon.	
	25/2/19.		Captain Browne proceeds on Leave, and Captain Squair assumes duties of Transport Officer during his absence.	
	27/2/19.		Report loss of Spare Rims, tyres and tubes from Cars during night. A dance was given for the Personnel, and was very successful.	
			Notes. It has recently been found necessary to guard the Hospital etc,vigilantly owing to the depredations of bands of burglars which infest this Area, many robberies have occurred in the Division and much property lost. This is a matter which has became urgent since the Armistice particularly since the arrival in the La Louvière Area. It is connected with the eagerness of the Civilian population to acquire food and clothes. The feeling between the Troops and the Civilians is nevertheless very friendly.	

[signature] Major,
A/O.C.1/2nd Highland Field Ambulance.
R.A.M.C. T.F.

160/3357

17 JUL 1919

3rd Aug F.O.

Aug. 1919

WAR DIARY
of 1/2nd Highland Field Ambulance, R.A.M.C.(T.F.)
INTELLIGENCE SUMMARY.

(Erase heading not required.)

Army Form C. 2118.

Vol. 47. Page 1.

Instructions regarding War Diaries and Intelligence Summaries are contained in F. S. Regs., Part II. and the Staff Manual respectively. Title pages will be prepared in manuscript.

Place	Date	Hour	Summary of Events and Information	Remarks and references to Appendices
BOIS-du-LUC	1-3-19.		Summer time came into operation.	
"	10-3-19.		Personnel of the Cadre chosen. Lieut. Colonel G. W. MILLER, D.S.O. proceeded to England for demobilization. Lieut. Colonel G. W. MILLER, D.S.O. addressed the Unit before leaving expressing the pride he had felt while in Command of an Ambulance which had invariably acquitted itself with so much credit and which had taken such a part in all the glorious actions fought by the 51st (Highland) Division in France. Captain A. C. LAING, M.C. proceeded to U.K. on 21 days leave. Major D. D. CRAIG, M.C. took over Command of the Unit.	
"	14-3-19.		Captain W. J. PROUD, Dental Surgeon was appointed Acting Quartermaster of the Unit.	
"	15-3-19.		At First Army Boxing Championship at DENAIN, FRANCE, the Welter Weight Championship Cup was won by No. 303051 Corporal A. CHRISTIE, of this Unit. Captain J.A.C.ROY struck off strength of this Unit on being posted to D.D.M.S. XXII Corps for duty.	
"	20-3-19.		The remaining retainable personnel of Other Ranks (4 O.R.) were sent to 32nd. Division, Germany.	
"	22-3-19.		Captain H. W. BROWNE, M.C. returned from leave.	
"	23-3-19.		Captain H. W. BROWNE, M.C. ordered to report to D.M.S. II Army for duty with Army of Occupation.	
"	27-3-19.		A "BAL D'ADIEU" was given by the Unit in the Salon Damien at Houdeng Goegnies.	
"	29-3-19.		Captain F. W. SQUAIR and Captain A. C. LAING, M.C., were struck off the strength of this Unit on being taken on the strength of R.A.M.C. No 1 Area.	
"	31-3-19.		The Divisional Rest Station ceased to receive patients from 31-3-19 owing to concentration of Divisional Cadres at MANAGE prior to entrainment.	

Army Form C. 2118.

WAR DIARY
of 1/2nd Highland Field Ambulance, R.A.M.C.(T.F.)
INTELLIGENCE SUMMARY

Vol. 47. Page 2.

(Erase heading not required.)

Place	Date	Hour	Summary of Events and Information	Remarks and references to Appendices
BOIS-DU-LUC	31-3-19.		NOTES:— The strength of the Unit on 31-3-19 is as follows:—	
			Officer Commanding. Major D.D.CRAIG, M.C.	
			Other Ranks. R.A.M.C. 60.	
			" " R.A.S.C.H.T. 16.	
			" " R.A.S.C.M.T. 4.	
			Total. 80.	

www.ingramcontent.com/pod-product-compliance
Lightning Source LLC
Chambersburg PA
CBHW080907230426
43664CB00016B/2745